IT'S NEVER JUST ANOTHER MONDAY

Blogging to engage and inspire across a vast organization

CARL S. ARMATO
NOVANT HEALTH CEO

It's Never Just Another Monday
by Carl S. Armato

Published by Novant Health
2085 Frontis Plaza Blvd., Winston-Salem, NC 27103
NovantHealth.org

ISBN 978-0-692-95413-3

This book is dedicated to my wife, Christi, my parents, Lucien and Leona, my children, Carly, John and Tyler, and my entire extended family. I will always be grateful for your love and support, which have allowed me to grow and thrive.

I also dedicate this book to my physician partners and Novant Health team members who deliver on the remarkable patient experience each and every day. Your dedication fuels me and I am honored to work alongside you.

Contents

DNA and building with teamwork

The marching brand and explaining the complex

Love of country and celebrating remarkable people

Date night and delivering service above and beyond

The iceman and drawing inspiration from family

Waking up love and supporting values on holidays

The tiny picnic and making healthcare remarkable

The White House and embracing the world around us

Foreword

This book is composed of selections from Novant Health CEO Carl Armato's team member blog from February 2012 to July 2017. Entries are published thematically, not chronologically, and content remains true to the original publication.

Author's preface

When I became president and CEO of Novant Health, I adopted communication as one of my top priorities. Our organization is large and complex, with more than 26,000 team members, 500 locations across four states and millions of patients and their families who come in contact with us every year. With eyes wide open, I began my role as CEO knowing that everyday challenges might tempt me to back-burner some of the personal characteristics I value in communicating, such as transparency, approachability and accessibility.

I rely on several strategies to communicate, but I hadn't used social media extensively prior to becoming CEO. With the promotion, I understood that effective, organization-wide communication required new tools. After all, I estimated the size of my new office at nearly 11.8 million square feet, roughly the combined space of all Novant Health hospitals, clinics and other facilities. I didn't plan to spend most of my time in the 300 square feet occupied by my desk and office furniture – I wanted to meet individuals where they worked. And even though I embraced that commitment, I knew that walking and traveling around our organization was a limiting tactic for getting to know staff and learning about their priorities.

On Feb. 24, 2012, I launched Carl's Corner, an internal blog published every Monday around noon. This book includes a sample collection of my posts over the past few years. The topics meander the healthcare landscape, from patient care to finances to politics and the human spirit. Many people inspired these posts: my family, Novant Health team members, patients, trustees and others.

The blog provides me with significant insight into our health system. Team members frequently react to my posts, with both positive and challenging feedback. The goal of creating a conversation is important to me, whether I receive encouragement or pushback. And yes, I read every blog comment.

One word best describes my blogging journey: conversation. While the blog words appear on a screen, the Monday morning posts have created more dialogue inside our organization. Team members are less bashful in approaching me or talking with me. If they don't receive enough information from their supervisors, they often ask me to blog about a topic. That makes everyone more accountable, and I believe Novant Health is better and stronger when people are having a conversation.

I hope you enjoy this book.

Section 1

The Wild West and transforming with leadership

"You're the blog guy!"

I have quite a few titles, like most people. Dad. Uncle. CEO. Friend. Neighbor. Hey You (for when I left my shopping bag at the store register).

While I was recently walking through a Novant Health facility and meeting with staff, one team member stopped me and commented, "You're the blog guy!" While I take my role as president and CEO very seriously, I wasn't the least bit offended by the informal greeting or by this individual's rather limited description of my scope of responsibilities. To the contrary, I was pleased that she knew about the blog and considered herself an avid reader of our online discussion on I-Connect.

I proceeded to ask if she ever made an online comment on the blog and she quickly affirmed, "Oh no, I'd be a little afraid to write something." We continued our discussion and it was very helpful. I explained to her that I read every comment and learn something new about our organization after almost every blog post.

For instance, I discover whether or not our leaders are communicating with staff about what's going on inside our organization and in healthcare. I once learned about a program that was not implemented in the way it was intended. I read about nurses, physicians and other staff who recognize both the successes and challenges of our organization. Most importantly, the blog lets me hear from a diverse group of staff from all communities that our health system serves.

When I was given the privilege to serve Novant Health as its president, I set out to meet with as many employees, physicians and board members as physically possible. People started casually referring to it as "Carl's listening tour," which was an accurate description of my intentions. I wanted to hear from people about what they're proud of and what they feel should change.

One of the consistent themes shared with me was the need to improve communication and to tell our story, both internally and externally. We have a lot of initiatives underway to address this important strategy, which includes reminding our managers and leaders that staff want to hear more from their own supervisor about what's going on inside our organization.

My listening tour taught me many things, including that I needed to expand my own communication with staff. And while I am committed to meeting face-to-face with team members as often as possible, I also realize that I need to supplement those meetings with more electronic and immediate methods of reaching people. This blog provides me with one more opportunity to communicate with you, to listen, to absorb your ideas, to hear about changes from your perspective, to be grounded by critical feedback and to be uplifted by comments that recognize all of the positive accomplishments by our staff and teams.

In closing, I'd like to thank the staff member who dubbed me the "blog guy." She reminded me that being a CEO requires the wearing of many hats and that increasing communication is well worth the time and effort.

Fired up for "no meeting Wednesdays"

It's official. Starting this week at Novant Health, we no longer hold meetings on Wednesdays. Yes, you read that right. This is a systemwide initiative that starts Wednesday, June 21, and it applies to everyone.

We spend a lot of time in meetings. It seems like all meetings are scheduled for an hour. Sometimes they end late because they start late. I'm often scheduled two to three meetings deep, and it's not unusual for my day to be back-to-back meetings with a break for lunch. I may still have those days, but no Wednesday meeting will be booked on my calendar.

Our goal in doing this is *not* to push more meetings and work into the other four workdays. It's to eliminate work so we can take a closer look at what's most important – our team members and patients.

Fewer meetings give us more time to role-model and highlight what's going well. To understand the barriers and remove them.

Oftentimes, the purpose of the meeting is an FYI that could easily have been shared another way: an email, a phone call or a quick conversation in the hall. This is true for every department throughout Novant Health.

The one possible exception here would be Wednesday meetings that are *totally* focused on engaging with team members, improving relationships, and encouraging individual growth and development. But under no circumstances should any meeting or huddle turn into a usual business meeting with agenda items.

We've reached the point where meetings often consume too much of our time and energy. Those two incredibly important factors need to be channeled elsewhere. Our time and energy need to go to supporting our team members and patients and walking alongside them – this is our work.

Fewer meetings give us more time to role-model and highlight what's going well. To understand the barriers and remove them. And to challenge our teams on how we can get better. These actions help us care for our team members so they can, in turn, care for our patients.

On Wednesdays, you can round on your team members and patients, shadow others in your department and beyond, and always find someone you can help.

If you haven't done so already, cancel Wednesday meetings on your calendar. Eliminate any meeting that doesn't add value so you can support those who do. Work with your leader on reprioritizing if you need to. Starting the day with an open schedule will allow us to engage more with one another and with our patients.

I can visit more of our facilities across the system now that I have a free day to do so. I look forward to seeing more of you out and about on Wednesdays, too!

Jordan is right for Novant Health's team

Most days I would tell you that I have the best job in the world because I love what I do. But Friday, March 9, was the day my kids decided I had the best job in the world. That's when we announced Michael Jordan had agreed to be a spokesperson for Novant Health. I tried to explain to them that there was a strategy and business objective to the relationship, but in their eyes it was just cool. And you know what? Having an international icon want to tell the world about how great and remarkable we are – well, it is pretty cool.

I've had the opportunity to talk to Michael on several occasions. He's really a nice guy and I have been impressed by how positive he is. I can relate to his positive attitude because I also try to see and search for the positive opportunities in every situation. I believe that is the mindset we need at Novant Health – right now – as we transform our healthcare delivery model to face the challenges that will come our way in the future. I believe a positive attitude and positive regard for others can overcome any obstacle.

We know that we will need to work differently in the future than we are today. Implementing one electronic health record for the system is just one example of how we need to change. We'll all be asked to make some changes as we transform every department in our organization. When you are given the opportunity to participate in transforming your department, there will be two choices – viewing the work negatively or positively. I encourage you to make the process a positive experience and participate in the transformation so your voices are counted. Focus on why we're changing, what goal we will achieve and how our patients will benefit. Be accountable, focus on the positive, and overcome the rest.

Yes, Michael Jordan has the right attitude for Novant Health. I am honored and proud he is on our team!

My lesson from the Wild West

During a brief respite and family vacation, I was a cowboy in the "Big Sky" state of Montana. If you're a skeptic, I have photos to prove it.

Actually, referring to myself as a cowboy, even a temporary one, probably insults every real cowboy in America. So instead I'll refer to myself as a guy who rode a horse and joined others from the city who wanted to experience some of the dust, ruggedness and history of our nation's great West.

One of my ranch experiences included an exhilarating, full-speed ride on horseback with a group of professional riders as well as a group of tenderfeet, which included me. I possessed a little more horseback riding experience than others – several hours as a teenager at camp and three days of riding during the current vacation. But not enough experience to join the rodeo or tame wild stallions.

As we began the ride, and as our speed increased, I felt confident and energized. The wind, the open spaces, the sound of hooves striking the hard earth – these were memories in the making. Then our horses increased their speed even more. And to my left I noticed one novice in our group losing control and composure. He kept riding, however, instead of using his alternatives, such as slowing down or asking for help. The ride ended abruptly for him, in a way vacations should never conclude.

The horse bucked and threw him. From my point of view, I saw him fly through the air and land in a way that most assuredly produced painful consequences. The dust settled and a real cowboy, who was also a fireman, came to his aid. The thrown rider's western experience ended with scrapes, cuts and 12 cracked ribs.

The incident shook me. Afterwards, I rode off to a quiet spot and reflected upon what had just happened. Before the ride began, we received great instructions, including advice that encouraged us to ask for help, to ride within our means and to rely upon the team of experts for guidance.

As hard as I try, I never completely separate work from play. Since our family vacation, that episode has galloped back into my thoughts several times as I worked safely at my desk. The incident reminded me how difficult it can be for some people to ask for help or to slow down and reassess their challenge. I think that hesitancy can happen to all of us, in every profession.

Horseback riding is incredibly dissimilar to operating an MRI scanner, charting at the patient's bedside or converting to an electronic health record. Yet, all require skill, attention and teamwork. We're faced every day with decisions about when to ask for help and when to invoke the advice of others. Slowing down is a viable option in order to learn how to safely accelerate in an environment that demands change.

I thoroughly enjoyed my experience out West and my time away with family. And now whenever my family comes across a western TV show while flipping through the channels, I always perk up a little and remember my ride.

He shared his despair with pride

While serving as a board member of a local United Way, I attended several fundraising events on behalf of the agency. I remember one particular luncheon that featured a guest speaker. He wasn't a dignitary or celebrity, at least as defined by traditional criteria. His impact on the audience and me, however, put him in a spotlight reserved for "stars."

The speaker had suffered from personal crisis and numerous problems, including mental health issues. His life imploded, including the loss of his family, and eventually his home became the inside of his car. As he told the story, I could visualize the past despair on his face – you could tell he'd always remember that miserable time in his life.

Addressing this luncheon crowd, though, was an individual

*He connected my role and my contribution to
a person who could have figuratively fallen
off the face of the earth. Yet he didn't.*

who changed his life with some help from strangers. He stood and spoke with pride on this day. And concluding, he shared with us his return to school and the joy from his current job – as a teacher. He thanked all of the social service agencies and their donors for believing that their efforts truly make a difference – large or small contributions, board members or volunteers, no matter what their motivation. Every good deed mattered to him.

If I had to select a single reason why I support our employee giving campaigns at Novant Health, that person's speech is a good one. He connected my role and my contribution to a person who could have figuratively fallen off the face of the earth. Yet he didn't.

With 26,000 team members at Novant Health, many of you know someone who has been helped by a social service agency or organization, maybe even a family member or a co-worker. Each one of us can make an impact in a lot of different ways, by volunteering, participating in a walk for a cure, donating money or coordinating a department effort during a holiday or special week. For instance, one Novant Health department recently celebrated its national professional recognition day by making hundreds of sandwiches for homeless clients and neighbors of the Urban Ministry Center. This type of commitment to serving others is embodied all around our health system.

Most of our facilities are currently conducting or planning to launch employee giving campaigns that support multiple agencies, a more focused cause such as United Way or the hospital's own foundation. I'm always impressed with the level of enthusiasm of staff who help coordinate these efforts and who volunteer to encourage fellow team members to donate to community agencies. For many people, it's not easy to ask others for money, yet every year staff sign up to take on that task.

When we get dressed every day and travel to work, we probably pass by individuals who are overwhelmed with hopelessness, crisis or a lack of the basic necessities to thrive. I owe this realization to the teacher who once lived in his car and willed himself to share his story with others. And I choose to donate to our employee giving campaign each year because I know that individuals and families will be served by the collective generosity from all of us. Thanks to each of you who contributes your resources of time and money to help those in need.

Healthcare ideas from bankers, sergeants and mouseketeers

Novant Health benefits from the talents of many long-tenured healthcare employees. And at one time during our organization's history, we believed "outsiders" – individuals from other businesses – probably wouldn't understand how healthcare works. Many hospitals, clinics and health systems across our nation operated with this bias.

We were both right and wrong.

We were right in believing that staff with healthcare experience form the backbone of our organization. However, we were wrong in our assumption that employees from outside of healthcare might not catch on to our unique and complicated industry. Fortunately, we have adjusted this attitude.

Our strategic sourcing division provides some great examples. Over the recent years, they've hired a number of professionals from other businesses: UPS, General Electric, Ingersoll Rand, Ford Motor Company and the U.S. Military. All of these organizations must swiftly and economically purchase supplies and move them efficiently to where their employees and customers need them. Our strategic sourcing division has made tremendous improvements, during a period of rapid growth and high demand for new solutions. And the infusion of staff from other industries has played a major role in reinventing the chain of identifying, purchasing and distributing the supplies all of you need.

Two recent additions to Novant Health also exemplify the diverse backgrounds of people who are joining our health system. Lynne Stuedli joined our information technology services (ITS) division six months ago as director of the project management office. She formerly worked at Disney, in addition to Knowledge Universe, which is part of KinderCare, and other non-healthcare companies. At Disney, she led a project management team for the parks and resorts group. In her tenure with Disney, Lynne worked on its 50th anniversary celebration, improving the customer experience and integrating marketing initiatives.

Jesse Cureton just recently joined Novant Health and our executive team. Jesse serves as our chief consumer officer after a long tenure with Bank of America, where he directed complex, corporatewide strategic initiatives and led the development of new customer solutions. Team members such as Jesse and Lynne bring in outside thinking that blends with the healthcare experience we have at Novant Health.

I'm also confident that many of our staff who joined us from other industries have respectively scratched their heads a few times, wondering why healthcare is operating the way it does. But we should all be thrilled that there's some "head-scratching" occurring at Novant Health. This diversity of ideas and rethinking of our processes makes us a better organization. We should never settle for tradition if there's an opportunity to explore a new way. Many of the companies and brands that you commented about in my last post – such as Apple, Amazon and Starbucks – have a lot of talented head scratchers inside their organizations who effectively challenge the way things have always been done.

If you're a head scratcher or a potential one – either with lots of years of healthcare experience or none – Novant Health needs your ideas. So do the patients and communities we serve.

Admitting staff scanned my iris

I recently visited Novant Health Presbyterian Medical Center and its admitting department. No, not for more stitches or family mishaps, like I've blogged about in the past. This time, I was being proactive with my healthcare experience, in addition to checking out firsthand the technology that scans a patient's eyes during the registration process.

Using the new equipment, admitting staff took photos of my iris and face, which are now stored and will be linked to our Dimensions electronic health record system. Like all patients, I had to agree to this scan. For individuals being admitted to the hospital, they barely notice the scan taking place, since the cameras are several feet away, unlike during a more intrusive eye exam.

Why add this new technology? Several good reasons, but I'll emphasize one: our vision and promise to make healthcare remarkable and safe for patients. For instance, while there may be only one Carl Armato living in the area, there are probably 20 or more Michael Smiths and other similar name combinations. And as you know from First Do No Harm training, accurately identifying patients avoids the creation of duplicate medical records, reduces mistakes and improves care. In addition, iris scanning during the admitting process decreases the threat of identity theft in our healthcare settings.

Naturally, some individuals are skeptical to change, but reactions so far have been very favorable. Patients have commented that they like the "contactless" process because they don't have to touch something that other people touch, as is the case in other admitting techniques that involve patient fingerprints or hand

... accurately identifying patients avoids the creation of duplicate medical records, reduces mistakes and improves care.

By proactively having this done, emergency staff and other healthcare providers can identify you in situations where you might be unconscious without other identification.

(palm vein) identification. In our environments, less physical contact keeps patients and staff safer during flu season. Also, several patients have jokingly requested scan copies for publishing on their social media sites.

I encourage staff to proactively visit admitting departments as our hospitals implement this new technology. Undergo the iris scan even if you're not planning to be hospitalized. By proactively having this done, emergency staff and other healthcare providers can identify you in situations where you might be unconscious without other identification. That means they'll know your health history, such as allergies, even without knowing your name. Adan, a patient access specialist, assisted me and enthusiastically showed off the new technology and capabilities. He walked me through the process and eye scan, impressing me with his professionalism and customer service.

So far, our hospitals in Matthews, Huntersville and Charlotte have operationalized iris scanning. In several weeks, Novant Health Rowan Medical Center goes live, with other hospitals following in the months ahead into 2014.

Iris scanning will cost approximately $1 million to implement systemwide. That's inexpensive when compared to converting to our electronic health record or building a new medical center. Yet a decision to spend even a hundred dollars should involve careful evaluation. In this case, the reasons were compelling and our patients will be safer because of it.

The world's best advertising? Word of mouth

Have you ever been somewhere outside the workplace when people ask you a medical question simply because you work in healthcare? I'm sure this happens to our physician partners and clinical team members all the time. But I'm a certified public accountant with an MBA – and surprisingly, many people want medical advice from me?! I've even had neighbors stop by my house or call me with questions about what to do for sick kids or parents. I refer these individuals to the world-class physicians and clinical and support teams at Novant Health.

Of course, it's no surprise people seek recommendations from Novant Health team members when they need a physician or health service. They want to go to the best place, and they see you as a reliable source for the inside scoop on whom they can trust to provide high-quality care and excellent service. And while advertising can help us create awareness of our services and our promise to deliver a remarkable patient experience, many people will ask friends and family as well. The most trusted source of information will come from our patients and team members.

Regardless of your position here at Novant Health, you play a role in shaping the content of word-of-mouth advertising about us. You do it through what you say to friends and family in person or through social media and how you interact with our patients and their loved ones while working. You serve as a brand ambassador and you also can help create them.

Being an effective brand ambassador includes taking advantage of simple openings to talk about us. When meeting new people, you might be asked where you work. Respond with an "ad" that could influence that person's future decisions about whom they will trust with their healthcare needs. Say with pride that you work for Novant Health and tell them how you're helping make healthcare remarkable through innovations like MyChart, online direct scheduling and extended hours at our medical clinics.

Creating brand ambassadors requires you to demonstrate our values and apply our standards of excellence. As the saying goes, actions speak louder than words, but I'm a strong believer that our words make a strong impression with patients as well. Make sure the actions and dialogue in your "ads" provide our patients with plenty of positive things to say when sharing their Novant Health experience with friends and family. Taking a few extra minutes with a patient who needs comfort could result in that person becoming a devoted brand ambassador for years to come.

To generate great word-of-mouth advertising, we need to be relentless in honoring our brand promise and recognize that the microphone is always on. What we say and do – whether at work or off the job – gets recorded in the memories of people who can become our brand ambassadors and help us grow. I'm confident that we have the world-class technology, team and care necessary to produce outstanding word-of-mouth ads that generate recommendations. I challenge all of us to be brand ambassadors and drive people to Novant Health.

Being open unlocks great conversations

I enjoy reviewing comments posted on my blog and take time to read all of them. Thank you for sharing your suggestions and concerns with me. The blog serves as one of the ways that Novant Health is building a culture of openness and transparency. We've used it to discuss both victories and setbacks – it's a place to celebrate our successes and learn from our challenges so we grow and improve as a team.

I value open and transparent dialogue and seek it when talking with others – whether on or off the job. Taking this approach keeps relationships honest and free of barriers. It makes sharing information easier, builds understanding, provides encouragement and creates a nurturing environment that fuels creativity and cooperation.

Having a culture that includes openness and transparency is necessary to create authentic personalized relationships – one of the elements in the remarkable patient experience. Patients learn to trust us when we open up and are clear in our discussions with them. Earning this trust helps us engage patients in the process of getting better and staying healthy.

You demonstrate a culture of openness when you ask patients for feedback. I've done this while rounding and picked up valuable insights. Seeking input helps you better meet patients' needs and conveys the clear message that you truly care about them. Being transparent with patients occurs when you take time to explain the purpose of a test or make sure they understand your role and what you're planning to do to help them.

As with our patients, the way we communicate plays a key role in how trust is developed within our team. To be effective, we need a willingness to discuss uncomfortable topics. This includes giving and accepting feedback respectfully and doing it with positive intentions – to resolve issues and achieve continuous improvement. Most people want the truth and are receptive to change when a trusted source points out something they should be doing differently.

Because effective communication is fundamental to our culture, the Novant Health executive team will now spend one day each month rounding and meeting with front-line team members throughout the organization. The goal is for executives to visit multiple locations in a set geographic area such as a hospital, group of physician clinics and nearby corporate office where they connect with as many team members as possible. Instead of traditional open forums, these meetings will be in informal, small group settings of 15 to 30 team members that make it easier to have more in-depth conversations.

Openness and transparency are traits that I want to see deeply embedded in our culture. I hope you will join me in applying them when interacting with patients, team members and others. Open up and be clear to experience the power of true communication.

And enjoy the outcome – authentic relationships based on trust, respect and understanding.

Following a blueprint to build our future

Building a house without a blueprint won't get you the results you want. A lot of work goes into the plan, because there's so much to consider. You have to think about finding the right site, laying a solid foundation and framing the walls. The plan also keeps you on track. Taking the scope of such a big project into account before you start can help make the process go smoothly. The same is true for our business strategy and imperatives – our blueprint for Novant Health.

It's important for the leadership of a growing healthcare system like Novant Health to step back and reflect on what's happened in our past. Last year, the executive team examined our successes and our challenges, and we explored what we need to do in order for Novant Health to grow and thrive in an industry that's constantly changing.

As the executive team reviewed healthcare trends, seven imperatives emerged to guide our planning and strategy for 2015 and beyond. I think it's also important that we understand what we mean by strategic imperative. Each imperative is an obligation that Novant Health must act on and respond to when changes are required by the healthcare industry, as well as for consumers and our patients.

These seven ambitious imperatives will be our priorities for the next few years.

• **High-performing, change-ready organization and resilient team** Novant Health will be responsive to the changing healthcare environment and adept at the large-scale changes required. Our team members will have the capability, adaptability and resilience to embrace and implement rapid change, ensuring that Novant Health continues to grow and thrive.

- **Population health: care models**
  Novant Health will continue to provide the remarkable patient experience to each individual patient, while developing a system of care that focuses on keeping our communities healthy.

- **Population health: financial management**
  Novant Health will understand the impact of cost and pricing of our services on our patients, team members and communities, enabling us to meet their needs. We will develop the competency and capability to do this in a financially responsible manner.

- **Technology optimization and business intelligence**
  Novant Health will leverage our technology and data and build our business intelligence to understand fully the needs of our customers and to deliver innovative healthcare solutions that create value for each customer segment.

- **Operational precision**
  Novant Health will continuously evaluate and improve our operational model to be aligned with the changes in healthcare and focus on efficiency and best-in-class practices, allowing us to thrive in a value-based system.

- **Innovative services, products and pricing**
  Novant Health will develop innovative healthcare products and pricing models that anticipate the needs of our patients, team members, communities and payers.

- **Industry leadership and growth**
  Novant Health will continue to grow to a multistate "super-regional" footprint to create economies of scale, attract talent, and fulfill an ambitious, industry-leading mission and vision.

These imperatives will keep us focused on what's important and what needs our attention. I'll tackle one imperative a week.

Nobody constructs a house without a blueprint. Likewise, we aren't going to grow Novant Health without a detailed plan.

*Ultimately, all of this planning allows us to provide
our patients and their families with simpler, more
affordable healthcare that is easier to access.*

Ultimately, all of this planning allows us to provide our
patients and their families with simpler, more affordable
healthcare that is easier to access. We've planned the work – now
it's time for us to work the plan.

Remarkable team members "write" and lead transformation

For about a year now, a team of nurses has been
researching, testing and trialing ways to transform patient
care and get nurses back to the bedside doing what they
do best – providing care to our patients.

A few weeks ago, I had the honor and privilege of meeting
some of the medical-surgical nurses, certified nurse assistants and
physicians at Novant Health Forsyth Medical Center who are
helping shape this new team model of nursing. Let me tell you – I
walked away from those meetings more certain than ever that we
can change the face of healthcare here at Novant Health.

These men and women demonstrated a passion for our values
of personal excellence and teamwork, as well as an extraordinary
level of professionalism and enthusiasm for this new nursing
model. What I saw and heard that day is truly remarkable. So, for
this week's blog, I want to share a few of the words and stories
from the nurses, certified nurse assistants and physicians I talked
to that day.

People such as Jenny, a registered nurse in orthopedics at
Forsyth Medical Center, who explained the benefit of the team
nursing model this way: "By the time I finish report and the
morning medications for my patients, I already know their names,

their children's names, where they work, and I even know how they like their coffee!"

WOW! There is no better definition of authentic personalized relationship in action!

But it didn't stop there. Every nurse, certified nurse assistant and physician I talked to that day literally buzzed with energy and excitement. On Forsyth Medical Center's innovation unit, Brenda, a registered nurse, told me that change usually comes from the top at Novant Health and then the nurses get to figure out what's wrong with the change. But now, she said, "You trust us. We get to write the change ourselves."

Joanne, a registered nurse in orthopedics, echoed Brenda's thoughts. "This transformation is the best and the worst," she told me. "This time, no one told us what to do. We had four guidelines that weren't negotiable and beyond that, it was wide open for us to create. As a nurse, being empowered to make these changes was scary and exciting at the same time."

When I asked Hannah, a registered nurse from Forsyth Medical Center's general unit, to share her experience with the new model, she told me, "We aren't afraid to try new things … we understand that not everything we try will work. Failure is OK because we learn from it and move on. We are a team."

Two of Forsyth Medical Center's ICS physicians were also on 9 NT that day. They emphasized the expanded physician/nursing partnership that exists in this new model and used team rounding as an example. I heard elements of safety, quality, authentic personalized relationships and clear communication as they described the daily team huddles where physicians and nurses talk about the medical, physical and emotional needs of each patient and family. It was clear to me that these physicians are passionate advocates for this new model and for the staff who are making it work.

Now don't get me wrong. The nurses I talked to also said there have been challenges, and that is normal when you start anything new. When I visited these units, it was just the second day with the new model. One nurse was very honest with me and said she was a little frustrated because it was her first day working with this new team approach. So I asked her, "What have you learned from your experience today?" She shared some lessons with me and summed it up by saying, "Tomorrow will be better. I know it!"

The three units I highlighted here today are just the first to test the new model. More units are going live this month and our goal is for all of the med-surg units to implement the new team nursing model by July.

More importantly, this same type of transformation is happening across the organization with every department and every team member. I look forward to sharing more stories of success with you in future blogs because the staff I spoke to that day reinforced my belief that we have innovative and creative thinkers who can transform the patient experience.

We must recognize the challenges and discomfort that come with transformation. But in the end, I challenge everyone to learn from the failures and frustrations, find ways to improve for the next day and keep building on our success. That is how we will create lasting change that will help us deliver the most remarkable patient experience in every dimension, every time.

Our homemade sauce is not a secret

I am fascinated how different audiences react to our story when I speak at conferences. Last month at a Press Ganey executive healthcare leadership conference in Orlando, I shared how Novant Health provides the remarkable healthcare experience by keeping the patient at the center of everything we do. And I explained how we do it as one unified team.

This time the C-suite and senior leadership audience keyed in on the unique relationship we have with physicians. And by the time questions and answers were over, my peers realized our physicians are truly helping us improve healthcare at Novant Health and they wanted to learn more.

Many organizations have partnered with their physicians across the United States, but few truly include them in every area of leadership like Novant Health has. I think the secret sauce to make this relationship truly successful is to give the physicians a voice and accountability in the strategy of the organization.

It wasn't that long ago when administrators and physicians worked in different worlds and certainly were not talking about how they could improve the business of healthcare. At Novant Health, we are committed to involving all key stakeholders, not just management. Our success depends on us working together. We don't tell our physicians what to do. We listen to them and they listen to us. It sets us apart from our peers. Every strategic discussion has physicians at the table, and every market partners a physician leader with an administrator. That too seemed to surprise the audience.

Now that physicians have a voice, they understand our strategy and vision; they're helping us make healthcare simpler, easier to access and more affordable. For instance, they've given up control of their schedules so patients can make online same-day appointments. We can't do it without their leadership and commitment to our promise.

Our physician leadership training program also captured the audience's attention. Physician burnout was one reason we invested in the program. For providers, the last decade has been tough, especially if you're practicing medicine. Many physicians are exhausted from dealing with healthcare's constant challenges and many frustrations.

We don't tell our physicians what to do.
We listen to them and they listen to us.
It sets us apart from our peers.

But, with this training, physicians started to recharge and reclaim their purpose. Physicians are no longer just thinking about what's going on within the four walls of their clinic. They're now thinking about how "we" can improve care for the Novant Health patient. They've refocused to put the patient at the center of everything they do. Their passion for healthcare has returned, and we thank Tom Jenike, MD, senior vice president of physician services, and Nicholas Beamon of the Center for Intentional Leadership for ensuring this program's success.

I also shared how we empowered our nursing team to overhaul processes to deliver better care. We brought in 50 nurses from across the system and gave them three criteria for change: practice at the top of their licenses, spend 70 percent of a 12-hour shift on direct patient care and reduce cost by 30 percent. As of today, 71 percent of a 12-hour shift is spent on direct patient care. The solutions to achieve this goal came to us through nurses. The nursing team decided to do all of their documentation in the room, as well as shift changes, so team members are in the room talking to the family and the patient about the care they are receiving.

They've also reduced cost by $55 million because of their team-based approach. And what it's done for the patient has been even more remarkable: 34 percent decrease in patient falls and 17 percent reduction in medication errors. Novant Health was successful because we tried something new. We thank all of our nurses for their outstanding efforts in leading the way for our patients.

I'll tell you what I told the healthcare executives: Novant Health is not waiting for someone else to take the lead. We're going to try new things to improve healthcare, and our physician leadership program is the perfect example of how we are doing that. Empowering our nurses to lead change also gave us great results. There aren't very many doing what we do and nobody is doing it better.

The secret to our success isn't just the sauce. It's our people who are working as one team: our physicians, nurses, the entire care team, pharmacists, environmental services technicians, volunteers, and the back office team along with the front office team. When it comes to delivering the remarkable patient experience, no team member is left behind. We're all in this together.

Our foundation supports everything we do

When team members join Novant Health, we begin their experience with new hire orientation. Besides providing a warm welcome, senior leaders and our corporate education and training instructors help these new team members get off to a fast start by enhancing their understanding of who we are and what's expected of them. The first topics discussed are at the foundation of everything we do – our mission, vision, values and promise.

The mission clarifies our purpose – why we exist. The vision communicates where we're heading as an organization and what we intend to accomplish. The values are the fundamental principles that drive our actions. And our promise is what we are committed to bring to our patients. Combined, they provide us with clear direction about our daily focus. That's why we reviewed them this year as part of our process in creating a new strategic plan for Novant Health.

- We reaffirmed our mission statement, as it is more relevant now than ever. We made a few modifications to our vision, values and promise to reflect how we're adapting to the changing healthcare environment.

All of these changes acknowledge the importance of personal excellence and teamwork in adapting to the challenging healthcare environment.

- In our vision, we simplified the message about who will deliver the most remarkable patient experience in every dimension, every time. Instead of including a specific mention of physician partners, the "we" in the vision statement is now defined as "the Novant Health team." When the vision was first created, we needed to make it clear that physician partners were included. Now, physicians are such an integral part of our team and strategy that we no longer need to make that distinction. I'm pleased to say that we're truly one team.

- For our values, we added "and inclusion" after "diversity" to more clearly define this value. This change emphasizes our belief that we'll be a stronger organization by engaging the unique life experiences, strengths and talents of each member. We also added a new value − courage − because it reminds us that we'll need to act boldly to make the changes necessary to deliver remarkable healthcare.

- We also reviewed and modified our promise even though it's relatively new. We created it last year when introducing the new Novant Health brand. The difference in our promise is slight yet significant. We rearranged the wording about what we bring our patients. Instead of leading with "technology," we now say "world-class clinicians, care and technology." The new version places our team first in how we intend to keep our promise to reinvent the healthcare experience to be simpler, more convenient and more affordable.

All of these changes acknowledge the importance of personal excellence and teamwork in adapting to the challenging healthcare environment. Through mid-December, I plan to use my blog to provide more detail about the changes and how they relate to each of us.

The first topic I'll cover is the importance of teamwork in achieving our mission and vision and in keeping our promise. Then, I'll elaborate about diversity and inclusion before wrapping up with a broader discussion of our new value of courage. As always, you'll have the opportunity to send me your comments and questions about these topics. I look forward to receiving your feedback.

By staying focused on our mission, vision, values and promise, we create an environment that makes everyone who works here feel remarkable, valued and part of a special team. We'll be coming to work every day full of purpose and conviction, knowing that our work truly makes a difference in our communities. Let's continue to build on our solid foundation that keeps us patient-centered and helps create a vibrant future for Novant Health.

Communities and patients need our courage

This is my final post on the changes we've made to our mission, vision and values. It's appropriate that we end with our new fifth value, courage. We're going to need it more than ever in 2015. Our values are important because they are the fundamental principles that drive our actions at Novant Health. The executive team added courage because we need to act boldly to pursue large initiatives that will allow us to improve care delivery.

First, I want to acknowledge that many of us act courageously in our jobs. To ensure patients' safety, for example, team members have found the courage to have difficult conversations to do the right thing. The courage we are talking about as a value is what we need as a systemwide team to improve the delivery of care. This commitment comes with many expectations balanced with just as many unknowns.

As an industry, healthcare tends to be risk averse. As an industry leader embracing change, Novant Health must find the courage to take more risks and try new things. We know we need to provide healthcare that is simpler, easier to access and more affordable. Adding courage as a value helps build the culture we need to essentially make decisions and pursue projects that may be difficult and make us uncomfortable. We have to get used to that feeling.

I have to tell you that what we have been doing is not easy. Novant Health has been leading the industry by showing people how healthcare ought to be delivered in a changing environment while keeping the patient at the center of everything we do. That's our commitment to the remarkable patient experience. Others are still too preoccupied with healthcare finances and cost cutting. We are focused on the entire healthcare experience – the patients, the community and our team members.

It's going to take courage to continue what we do on a larger scale. Creating a focused culture of wellness for our team members will require courage. Choices and Champions will require courageous conversations with our patients and their families and at home with each of our families as well. It takes courage for primary care providers to talk to parents about why antibiotics are not the best treatment for children with an upper respiratory infection.

These pursuits have great potential for making a positive impact on how we deliver care. Yet what those outcomes will be are currently unknown and daunting. We also may not always succeed when we act boldly, but we'll never know unless we have the courage to try. If we eventually need to regroup and reassess, that's OK, too. That's what being courageous is all about.

When I share the Novant Health story at conferences, I start by talking about our mission, vision, values and brand promise because these, more than anything else, tell others exactly who we are. They also are the foundation for our future. Let us find the courage to be open to new ways of thinking so we can boldly improve the remarkable patient experience.

I'd make a lousy undercover boss

D id you ever have one of those days that didn't go very well? The type of day that you'll remember for a very, very long time?

I experienced one of those days not too long ago. It ended better than it began.

While at a nearby farm, I had a mishap. My injury resulted from a blow to the head; from a large laceration, I was bleeding enough to make everyone with me nervous while we sped to the emergency room at Novant Health Huntersville Medical Center.

Since it was my day off, I arrived looking very un-CEO-like. A blood-soaked, makeshift bandage was wrapped around my head, topped off with a baseball cap. As I walked into the emergency department, a triage nurse met me, briefly sized me up and, before I could say very much, exclaimed, "If you're trying to play *Undercover Boss* today, I recognize you!"

Nine stitches later, along with other care and treatment, I left the hospital. And if I were to ever contemplate being on the popular CBS television show, my recent emergency experience proved that I'm probably not a good candidate for a network appearance on *Undercover Boss*.

My family and I would like to thank the entire emergency room team who provided me care and comfort during my impromptu visit. I'd also like to acknowledge the triage nurse who so playfully, but respectfully lightened the moment with her revelation about how I was failing in my undercover work.

All of us can play a role in making healthcare remarkable. When you use a Novant Health service, whether planned or unplanned, whether in crisis or during a routine health checkup, please share your feedback with the units, departments, centers

If every team member prioritized sharing feedback, we'd benefit from tens of thousands of ideas and suggestions each year.

and clinics. If every team member prioritized sharing feedback, we'd benefit from tens of thousands of ideas and suggestions each year. Your ideas, or kudos shared about your experience, are priceless. Also, if you're not sure how to share your feedback, ask your own manager for direction.

When you visit a Novant Health facility, you're likely to be less conspicuous than me. And together, by sharing ideas and feedback, we can all contribute to improving care for those we serve.

She spells it R-E-S-P-E-C-T

I want to warn you: Some people may not like this particular blog post. I hope it's only a few staff members.

Once you hear Aretha Franklin's classic song "Respect," it's difficult to stop replaying the melody and the title inside your head. The specific word "respect" is not one of Novant Health's four core values, but the principle is woven through the quartet of compassion, teamwork, diversity and personal excellence.

A few weeks ago someone brought to my attention that several team members were calling Novant Health human resources staff to voice their displeasure about a change in health insurance benefits. The callers chose to yell and curse at their fellow co-workers.

I'm realistic. All of our communities have people who refuse to act respectfully in dealing with others. I notice it at checkout counters or waiting in line. Novant Health is a large organization and is often a reflection of our communities. And unfortunately, we sometimes hire people who don't bring to work all of the values we seek.

Most importantly, no staff member should have to tolerate any form of abuse from another staff member. Everyone should expect me to prioritize this basic level of respect for each other. I have held people accountable for disrespectful behavior and I will continue to do so in the days and years ahead. If we can identify the individuals who disrespectfully confronted our HR benefits staff, we will expect their managers to follow up and take the appropriate steps, just as if a staff member had treated a patient or family member in the same manner.

Please don't misinterpret my feelings about this. We need to celebrate team members who practice with a questioning attitude. All of us should feel comfortable asking questions, sharing opinions and expecting answers, even during disagreements. However, we must provide all feedback respectfully as we engage one another.

I understand that health insurance and benefits can be complicated. And yes, we make changes to ultimately keep our employee benefit plan as strong as possible. No one, however, will be allowed to verbally abuse another person, no matter how complicated the issue might be.

The recent examples of verbal abuse arose over the change in spousal coverage, which now states that a Novant Health team member's spouse who has access to another company's employer-sponsored medical coverage is no longer eligible for Novant Health's plan. We made this change to keep our own plan as viable and strong as possible. Insuring another company's employees places a disproportionate burden on our organization's benefit plan. For the most part, our staff understands this change, but some staff members are unhappy because their spouse's employer may not offer benefits like ours.

My blog is intended to serve as a dialogue. When I became president, I toured the organization and listened to as many staff as possible to learn about your priorities. A major theme I heard from all of you focused on improving communication. This blog is one example of my commitment to this important goal. I promise not to utilize this resource to lecture people, especially when the intended audience for this post is a small group. I also hope you will acknowledge that this might have been a good exception.

Section 2

The happiness ripple effect and prioritizing our health

It's time to merge my job with part of my private life

I've lived with type 1 diabetes for a long time. I was diagnosed at 18 months of age with juvenile diabetes. I'm confident my family and physicians would describe my disease as "under control." Many of you understand how challenging this can be.

I've been managing my disease for as long as I can remember. It started when my parents noticed that, as a toddler, I ate way too much. They also noticed several other unusual symptoms that led to testing, which revealed a blood sugar level of over 800 – approximately eight to nine times what would be considered a healthy and normal result.

As I grew up, my family rallied around me and supported my personal efforts to control diabetes. My father was a big believer in exercise and my mother prepared meals as if everyone who ate at our house had diabetes. They also believed in helping me enjoy childhood and participate in "kid things." If a birthday party was planned for later in the day, my parents would always remind me to exercise ahead of time so that my body could better handle the cake, without the frosting. For Halloween, every house I went to offered me fruit instead of candy. I proudly returned home with the heaviest candy bag in the neighborhood! And because of adaptations like these during my childhood, I felt included, not excluded.

That feeling of inclusion didn't seem as apparent in other kids with diabetes I knew during my upbringing. While attending a two-week camp for 10- to 12-year-old children with diabetes, I met others who struggled with their disease. Their families treated them as if they were made of eggshells or had a handicap that couldn't be controlled. I sometimes experienced that coddling from well-intentioned people outside of my inner family circle.

For instance, after one of my middle school basketball coaches learned about my diabetes, I started playing less. My performance in games had been improving; in fact, I was the starting point guard, but my playing minutes kept decreasing. My coach constantly asked if I was OK and if I needed to rest. I realize it's a natural instinct for adults to protect kids; plus, during my childhood, diabetes was more of an enigma to many people. Thankfully, that has changed with more research and education about diabetes. As a young teen, I even played a small role in fostering a better understanding about diabetes. My pediatrician asked me to talk with newly diagnosed adolescents about coping with diabetes and balancing daily management of the disease with sports and the fun parts of life. I remember my father's quote from an early age: "You can realize your dreams with diabetes – you just have additional planning and a few precautions to consider."

Over the years, our medical centers and physician clinics have advanced wellness in our communities with innovative programs that have reached out to individuals, neighborhoods and entire towns. Yet, to date, as a unified Novant Health, we have not adopted a systemwide community health initiative. That will change later this week when Novant Health publicly announces an ongoing community outreach project related to diabetes.

More specifically, we will focus on prediabetes, obesity and high blood pressure. Prediabetes is a medical condition affecting one in three Americans 20 years of age and older. The overwhelming majority of people with prediabetes are unaware they have it. Despite the fact that most health experts consider it a national epidemic, prediabetes has slowly crept up on society and now threatens 79 million Americans, more with each passing year. Prediabetes is a precursor – it almost always turns into type 2 diabetes in 2 to 10 years if individuals don't change their health habits. However, many people with prediabetes can prevent or delay diabetes and, in some cases, return their blood sugar levels to normal.

People who are obese are more likely to have high blood pressure, and that combination puts them at a greater risk for

... the millions of people with undiagnosed prediabetes have the very real opportunity to prevent their condition from advancing into diabetes.

heart disease, stroke, diabetes and other chronic conditions. Since these conditions are often linked, we've decided to help our communities know their personal risks and help them live healthier lives.

My blog post today isn't designed to share all of the project's details – keep watch for future communications and ways to become involved and share the message.

In the past, I've considered blogging about my diabetes but chose to be more private about it. Now, I have a renewed motivation – I believe in this community outreach project and want everyone to share the pride in our efforts.

I will continue to manage my disease for the rest of my life, but the millions of people with undiagnosed prediabetes have the very real opportunity to prevent their condition from advancing into diabetes. And helping individuals in our communities prevent that from happening is worthy of our promise to help people stay healthy. And it's worth my time to talk about it and share my story.

Making this a summer of renewal

S ummer is officially here, but many of us already have been enjoying the season on trails, in the woods or at the beach. And pursuits like those are so important, because they're opportunities to get outdoors and invest in ourselves and our relationships – to refresh, renew and reconnect.

I've always been an outdoors person. Many of you know I love riding horses and engaging in other outdoor activities. I grew up in a Louisiana family that loved to gather around the grill and picnic under the trees by the bayou. I enjoy getting outside on the tractor, even cutting the lawn – just about anything, so long as it's outside. Wherever you live, even the simplest of activities – throwing a Frisbee in a park with the kids, gardening, walking the neighborhood and chatting with neighbors – take on an extra importance this time of year. My family has a longstanding tradition of heading to the beach in the summer – not just immediate family, but a big group that includes my mom, mother-in-law and brothers. We enjoy time spent catching up, telling stories, walking the beach and fishing.

Summer is the time many of us naturally gravitate to the lawn, mountains, local parks and beaches – and to spend time with those important to us. The health benefits of time spent in nature are well-documented. Just one example: One recently published scientific study found that people who took a walk in a natural setting showed healthier, less-stressful thinking patterns and greater mental well-being. Who couldn't use a little greater well-being and a little less stress in life?

I don't know about you, but anytime I can unwind outside with friends and family, it pays enormous dividends on the job. We are more alert, full of energy and ready to deliver remarkable care to patients and engage with fellow team members when we make time to enjoy nature and reconnect with people in our personal lives.

In the communities where our team members live, there are beautiful greenways, state park trails and city parks. This summer try an activity that's new to you. You might enjoy kayaking, hiking, swimming, or maybe even bird-watching like our own chief medical officer, Tom Zweng. You can get your daily steps in, improve your health and enjoy the outdoors in the company of family and friends. Take time this summer to replenish your spirit, enjoying the natural world and making deeper connections with others. It's a gift we can give to ourselves.

I'd love to hear what you plan to do outside this summer. Share your stories and suggestions of healthy ways to enjoy the summer. We can all pick up a few new ideas to try this season!

The ripple effect of happiness

I'm a big believer in the value of choosing a positive attitude and being optimistic. Our frame of mind can have a big influence on our lives, both personally and professionally. That's why I am excited that *The Happiness Advantage* by Shawn Achor is our book for this year's Novant Health Reads.

The selection comes from Tom Jenike, MD, our chief human experience officer, and Melissa Perrell, our leader for Novant Health Reads. They chose this book to help foster team member engagement. It's no secret healthcare is a very rewarding and often challenging profession. We know we need to care for ourselves, just like we care for our patients. To deliver the best possible care, we need to foster a culture that promotes wellness, engagement and resilience. Tom and Melissa believe this book can help us do that.

Evidence shows that if we change our mindset so we can be happier and more positive, it can give us a richer, more fulfilling life. Happiness and optimism actually fuel performance and achievement, giving us the competitive edge that Mr. Achor calls "the happiness advantage." Being happier in our personal lives leads to more productive professional lives. We engage more with our patients and are more aligned with our mission, vision and values. That's pretty impressive.

Our hope is that this book will help us unleash our full potential by providing us with tools to foster a positive mindset. The book highlights strategies such as practicing daily gratitude and reconnecting to a higher purpose for our work life. For us at Novant Health, that could mean rediscovering why we chose to work in healthcare.

Over the years, as my career has taken me through different industries and locations, I've witnessed how happiness can have a ripple effect. Anyone with a smile and a great attitude has the potential to create an environment that generates happiness. And happier environments are more likely to foster innovation, creativity and remarkable outcomes – positive energy that is contagious for all team members and patients.

Please join us in reading *The Happiness Advantage*. We've distributed 15,000 books. After we read the book, we can share in discussion groups our thoughts about what we've learned. I know many stories will be shared and questions answered, including this one: "How has reading this book affected our lives?"

Here's to opening another book to learn and grow together as healthcare professionals and team members.

Yes, we need a national day for this!

All of us know that exercise is an essential part of living a healthy life. Throughout my childhood, my parents made sure I exercised every day to help keep my blood sugar level stable because I have type 1 diabetes. Consequently, I have never really looked at exercise as something I have to do. It's something I want to do because it's part of who I am.

Last Wednesday, a lot of you joined me as we went outside to celebrate National Walking Day, sponsored by the American Heart Association. As board chairman of the local American Heart Association in Charlotte, I couldn't be prouder of the potential of such a simple initiative to improve the health of so many.

Anyone with a smile and a great attitude has the potential to create an environment that generates happiness.

I saw some of you venture out together for a walk before your shift started, while others walked during the lunch hour. I hope you enjoyed the walk as much as I did. My wife, Christi, often surprises me by stopping by the office for lunch, and we usually grab a walk together after we eat.

Walking is a great way to get exercise. Remember, exercising does not mean you have to focus on the number of calories burned or miles logged – nor should exercise require special skills and mandatory training time. It's about getting your body moving, and walking happens to be the easiest form of exercise that most of us can do. Pretty much all we need is a pair of comfortable shoes.

More walks would be good for our minds and bodies. Walks let us take a break, breathe in some fresh air and enjoy the scenery outside. I've always walked a great deal around my neighborhood, especially this time of year when the dogwoods and redbuds are in full bloom and birds are singing.

Here's my challenge to you: Let's find 15, 20 or 30 minutes to walk two or three days a week. And if you're doing this at work, we have great walking trail maps with distances measured for 13 of our medical centers.

Let's take our yearly celebration of walking and make it part of the daily life we enjoy.

I hope to see you out there.

That "one person" is you

When we talk about Novant Health existing "to improve the health of our communities, one person at a time," the "one person" should include you and me. That's because actions are louder than words. People will pay more attention to our message when they see us living it.

We focused on this need to "walk the talk" at the recent meeting for all Novant Health leaders, recognizing that our commitment to population health begins with the wellness of our own team. We discussed ways to create a healthy culture that leads to healthy lifestyles and a healthy workforce.

Leaders were encouraged to support their teams by creating a positive work environment and focusing on our values of teamwork, compassion, diversity and personal excellence. This kind of environment contributes to happiness. And studies show there is a natural synergy between being happy and being healthy. The happier you are, the healthier you tend to be; and, conversely, the healthier you are the happier you tend to be. And, happy, healthy people tend to be high performers.

While culture plays a significant role in how well and how long we live, the most dominant factor is individual behavior – the choices we make daily. As members of the healthcare industry, I'm sure you've seen many examples of the painful and destructive consequences of making bad choices.

I understand this connection and apply it to my life. As someone diagnosed at 18 months of age with type 1 diabetes, I need to pay close attention to my diet and make time for exercise. While the impact for me is severe if I fail to properly manage my eating and exercise habits, every person suffers negative effects if he or she ignores the requirements of a healthy lifestyle.

Exercise is hard work and eating properly can be difficult for many of us, but the benefits are worth it. I learned the value of exercise from my father. He took time to exercise and encouraged me to follow his example. I kept this family tradition alive by exercising with my children. While working out, we chatted about what was going on in their lives. It was a great way to stay in shape and remain connected as a family.

Many people say they don't have time to exercise. I understand that problem because I'm very busy. That's why I schedule my exercise time. I encourage you to do the same. Make your health a priority by reserving space on your calendar for exercise.

With the summer months coming, it's the perfect time to get started. The warm weather makes it easier to get outdoors for a walk or run. And you can adopt healthier eating habits as it's the prime season for fresh fruits and vegetables.

We all need to bring our best effort to the organization every day and that requires us to take care of ourselves. As part of our commitment to population health, we have a responsibility to set a good example by literally walking the talk. Make a commitment to set an example for our communities by making changes today to model a healthy lifestyle. The "one person at a time" to most benefit from your actions will be you.

Your freedom to eat wisely

On Friday, July 4, we celebrate the day in 1776 when Congress officially adopted the Declaration of Independence – a monumental step in securing the freedoms we continue to enjoy. When John Hancock signed it, he used a large, bold signature and exclaimed, "There, I guess King George will be able to read that." His defiant act for the cause of freedom became so well-known that more than two centuries later people still use the expression "give me your John Hancock" when asking you to sign something.

On Independence Day, I hope your actions serve as a bold "signature" that others will be able to read whether you are on or off the job. As with other holidays, it's a chance to draw extra attention to our mission to improve the health of communities, one person at a time.

For those of you working that day, it's the perfect time to deliver the most remarkable patient experience, in every dimension, every time. Unfortunately, health challenges never take holidays, which means many people will be turning to us for help in getting better and staying healthy. They are likely to feel frustrated by their need for medical treatment that prevents them from celebrating the day with family and friends. Through the care and comfort provided, you deliver a clear message that you will be there for them in the way they need. Your commitment to put patients first is appreciated by them and me. I thank all of our team members who will be working on the Fourth of July and other holidays.

If you are taking time off, your day might include cookouts and parties where you have the opportunity to walk the talk about our commitment to creating an epidemic of health and wellness. Instead of splurging, you can serve as a role model by practicing moderation in how much you eat and drink and picking healthy options. I know that's difficult when faced with so many items on traditional holiday menus that are high in fat and sugar. But you can do it.

Here's some excellent nutritional advice from Ashley Riggs and Amanda Smith in Novant Health wellness and condition management:

- Begin with foods such as a green salad, raw fruit and veggies that are low in calories but make you feel full (go easy on the salad dressing).

- Limit your intake of high-calorie foods, including chips and dips, crackers, bread and desserts.

- Select lean entrees – salmon, grouper, shrimp or chicken breast with the skin removed.

- Go light on the drinks and try ice water with cucumber slices or fresh lemon. Other beverage options include sparkling water with a dash of 100 percent fruit juice and black or green unsweetened tea. If you drink alcoholic beverages, alternate with an 8-ounce glass of water.

Instead of splurging, you can serve as a role model by practicing moderation in how much you eat and drink and picking healthy options.

- Enjoy a summer dessert – fresh strawberries with angel food cake, grilled peaches or pineapple, and fresh, cold watermelon.

While protecting your body by what you put into it, remember that heat- and sun-related illnesses can occur quickly and in any age group. To avoid sunburn and the less common but extremely dangerous heat stroke, limit your sun exposure to early morning hours and late afternoon/early evening hours, use SPF 15 or greater sunscreen, wear sunglasses and a wide-brimmed hat, and stay hydrated. And there are many more tips I could provide related to water and boating safety as well as safe driving, but you know them well and I don't need to elaborate.

Our challenge usually isn't a lack of knowledge – it's the willpower to break old habits. But we are in control of our choices and can declare independence from the past and start new, healthier traditions. I encourage you to use the Fourth of July to exercise your freedom to choose what is best for your health for that day and beyond.

It's hiding behind the fat content

In some of my recent blog postings, I've focused on the importance of making healthy choices because both your actions and advice to patients support our commitment to creating an epidemic of health and wellness. Before I move on to other topics, I want to make one additional point about our daily decisions that play a significant role in how well and how long we live. Today's topic is the problem with consuming too much sugar.

When consumers began seeking more low-fat or fat-free options, food and beverage manufacturers added more sugar to their products to compensate for the taste change that occurred when removing fat. As a result, many products may appear to be healthy based on the fat content, but the high level of sugar makes them a poor choice for someone trying to maintain a healthy weight.

To avoid consuming too much sugar, pay attention to food packaging labels and nutritional information posted in restaurants or on their websites. I believe you will be surprised by how much sugar is in certain food and beverages. And when reviewing that information, you should note the serving size. Often something that appears to be one serving is being presented as two or more. That means you need to at least double the grams of sugar and calories listed on the label.

The problem with consuming so much sugar is that it can lead to being overweight or obese, which raises the risk for type 2 diabetes, heart disease and stroke. But don't think that merely switching from sugary drinks to water or diet sodas will be enough to avoid overindulging in sugar. If you read labels on beverages and food, you'll find there is a lot of sugar in many products. For example, a popular sports drink has 120 calories and 29 grams of sugar in a 16-ounce bottle. And a leading brand of yogurt promoted as being 99 percent fat-free has 31 grams of sugar and 180 calories in a 6-ounce serving.

Catherine Rolih, MD, endocrinologist and medical director of the Novant Health diabetes service line, advises her patients to read labels carefully and to consider rejecting food and beverages with sugar listed as one of the top two or three ingredients. But she warns that sugar is often presented under different names such as high-fructose corn syrup or cane sugar.

Besides being wary of consuming too much sugar, Dr. Rolih recommends monitoring carbohydrate intake because starches metabolize into sugar. Food and beverage labels provide information about the amount of carbohydrates per serving size and what those carbs represent in terms of a recommended daily allowance. She also encourages building diets around good carbs such as fruit, vegetables and whole grains while avoiding bad or "concentrated carbs" such as candy and sugary drinks. She also endorses selecting good fats such as olive oil and avoiding bad fats listed on labels as trans fats or unsaturated fats.

*I challenge you to make decisions based on
their effect on your health and encourage others
to do the same.*

A healthy diet is only part of an effective approach to weight management, with exercise being equally important. Through diet and exercise, you and your patients can lead a sustainable healthy lifestyle that helps manage existing health issues and avoid the complications created by poor choices. I challenge you to make decisions based on their effect on your health and encourage others to do the same. It's a great way to improve the health of our communities, one person at a time.

Being bold for our communities

It's a bold claim, but I believe Novant Health can improve not just the health of every individual, but the health of an entire community. That's the aim behind population health, our second strategic imperative.

Population health: care models – Novant Health will continue to provide the remarkable patient experience to each individual patient, while developing a system of care that focuses on keeping our communities healthy.

We will build and scale the clinical capability and needed infrastructure (manpower, processes, technology, structure) to manage "enrollee" health. We will test our model before we scale it. For instance, we are piloting an "extensivist clinic" at Novant Health Huntersville Medical Center now. We believe we can safely discharge certain patients from the hospital earlier and schedule them for daily follow-up with Novant Health Inpatient Care Specialists, our hospitalist group, in our outpatient infusion center. If the trial is successful, we want to expand it across the system.

We will deliver results in existing at-risk arrangements, starting with our own Novant Health team base. The population health model starts with us. We spent more than $200 million on our team members' healthcare last year and our goal is to reduce that cost this year. We have to show people that we can reduce our own spending and improve our own health.

We will determine the high-priority/high-leverage episodes that need to be redesigned across the continuum, shifting focus toward prevention or management versus urgent and acute utilization. We will better manage our patients with chronic diseases and conditions – diabetes, congestive heart failure and asthma – to keep them healthy and out of the hospital. Coordinating their care will be key.

We will develop partnerships around critical elements of the population health continuum that Novant Health lacks, either on a service-specific or geographic-specific basis. We will work with others in the community (long-term care facilities, free clinics) to provide better care, such as skilled nursing facilities for many of our patients who may be residents or who may be recovering from joint surgery.

This is a whole new world for Novant Health, and I really want you to think about what we are saying. We're not going to wait for people to show up sick at the physician office, the urgent care clinic or the emergency room. We are going to be proactive. And the key to our population health success is the integrated team of nurses, pharmacists, social workers, dietitians, health coaches and referral coordinators, also known as the care coordination team, working together with our providers to encourage wellness and preventive care and to manage existing conditions to slow or reverse the progression of disease. All of them are working to keep the individual person healthy and often take different approaches in doing so.

Population health's team approach recently helped a patient whose health could have been at risk. A care coordinator discovered the discharged patient had failed to take key medications, including the blood thinner Coumadin. A check of the discharge summary found the prescription was sent to a mail order pharmacy, which the person did not use. The primary care physician was alerted via MyChart, and, within minutes, the right prescription was called into the pharmacy.

The right care was provided because someone reached out to the patient and solved the problem. Similar conversations happen every day where we have integrated core teams in north Charlotte, Winston-Salem, northern Virginia and Thomasville. It's our new approach to delivering remarkable healthcare while keeping people healthy, and we're doing it one patient at a time.

Unplug yourself

These days it's hard to find a school that doesn't schedule a spring break during the months of March or April. It's a week to shut down and check out. It gives young adults and teachers a break from each other and, hopefully, brings them back more focused to finish the year strong.

At Novant Health, we also think that taking a break from work is pretty important, and we'll even pay you to do it. Providing the remarkable patient experience is very rewarding work, but it can also be demanding. All of us know work can be very stressful, so being able to unwind comes with benefits of improved health and well-being. I encourage you to schedule your paid time off now. And if not now, then start thinking about the best time for you to do so.

Planning ahead is essential because we need to navigate one another's calendars to provide sufficient coverage. Everyone can't schedule time off now in ActiveStaffer, but you can start planning the year. In some cases, I realize there are designated times when some can't leave. For example, for those working on Dimensions launches, we need to have team members available during go-lives. Even the executive team coordinates schedules so we have coverage, just like every other team needs to do. I also have limitations as to when I can plan my vacations, which will never come during a Novant Health board meeting.

Like you, I need to unplug from work, and I've booked two weeks off. I'm already looking forward to my family's annual trek to the North Carolina beach for a week of relaxing. We've made this trip for many years, and the older my three kids get, the harder it can be to get our schedules to align. But we make it work because we plan ahead. The other annual trip on my calendar is a visit to my family in Louisiana. I look forward to seeing my mom and catching up with my extended family and friends. I'm a big believer in the power of vacations to replenish and recharge. Time off is good for me, my family and the people I work with.

You don't have to spend a week at the beach to reap these benefits. A long weekend at home several times a year can be just as good. The important thing is to take care of yourself, and part of that routine should be paid time off away from your job. You've earned it. Please take it.

Here's another suggestion: Cut the communication cord. I challenge you to totally disconnect from your job. No emails. No voicemails. No texts. If that's too hard to do, then limit your check-in to once a day or, better yet, every other day. Trust me. Your team will be OK.

Often, if you don't plan your days off, then you don't take time off. That's what we want to avoid. Book your time off now for the rest of the year. There's always going to be more work that needs to be done. If you have scheduled paid time off, the work can wait or you should have someone who can cover while you're out.

The important thing is to take care of yourself, and part of that routine should be paid time off away from your job. You've earned it.

We need you to take care of yourself. The odds are good that after you take your time off, you'll come back to work better prepared to take care of business.

You really, really need this person in your life

For many, ringing in the new year is often synonymous with making a resolution. Leading the self-improvement list are losing weight, spending less and enjoying life more. I'd like to throw another suggestion into the mix. Make sure we all have a primary care provider (PCP).

A PCP really can make a difference when it comes to our health. That's what I heard every time I got an update last year from our population health team as that group worked to connect team members with Novant Health providers. People who have a primary care provider and get annual wellness checkups receive better quality of care. They also tend to be healthier and happier with their care.

And if you stop and think about it, this makes sense. The PCP is our point of entry into the healthcare system and the person who then oversees all of our care. These providers make sure we get the right care at the right time, and that starts with preventive care – physical exams, vaccinations, bloodwork, mammograms, blood pressure checks and colonoscopies.

The PCP expertly manages acute and chronic illnesses as well, including conditions such as the flu, sinus infections, diabetes, high blood pressure, heart disease, depression and many more. If we need a specialist, the PCP will recommend one.

I also learned last year that patients with a PCP miss fewer workdays, avoid costly duplicated tests and save precious time when health issues do arise. And ultimately, receiving the appropriate primary care reduces our overall healthcare costs.

I faithfully see my PCP for regular checkups, usually four times a year, and this relationship has strengthened over time. My family physician knows my history. The fact that I have diabetes raises my risk for serious health problems, so my doctors keep close tabs on how I'm doing, especially my A1C levels.

My appointments usually end with this comment: "Carl, do you have any other questions for me?" Not being bashful, I usually don't, because I've asked all of them already. Then my PCP's parting thought is: "Call me, or send me a MyChart message, if you think of any." And I will.

Our latest population health report indicated that about 90 percent of team members and their dependents have a PCP listed on the health record. I would love to see that number hit 100 percent. But more importantly, I would love to see our team members engage with their PCP annually to ensure better health and to catch conditions earlier. It's a goal that's attainable. We just need to make it a priority this year.

Here's to a healthy 2016 for you and your families.

He got cheered; now Gerald is cheering others

Many of us have a vague, nagging desire to live a healthier lifestyle. Some of us turn those wishes into action. But sustaining good choices over the long haul – that can be tough. And that, said Gerald Hedrick, is exactly why we need friends and colleagues who can surround us with encouragement when our own willpower weakens.

Gerald, 58, a heating, ventilation and air conditioning technician with Novant Health shared services, was nominated as a healthy team member role model for the determination he's shown in forging a path to wellness. But it's a path that Gerald says he's not walking alone.

It all started about five years ago when Gerald's doctor told him his numbers didn't look good: Cholesterol and blood pressure were too high and Gerald was prediabetic. And Gerald has a side catering business, so he was surrounded by food.

How many of us have been at precisely this place, seeing a less-healthy future stretch before us, daunted by the long odds against making a change? It's easy to feel defeated before we even begin.

Here's what Gerald did: He joined colleagues walking at lunch. They looped around Novant Health Huntersville Medical Center, a one-mile path. They added a second lap. Then a third.

Gerald got a Fitbit and shared the data with his physician. He found new ways to cook – adding herbs and cutting salt, cutting fat and adding flavor. All the steady, small changes paid off. He averages 16,000 steps a day and has lost weight. He was able to reduce his blood pressure medicine. And he's no longer prediabetic.

In November, Gerald walked the Novant Health Thunder Road 5K with his wife, Dot, practice manager at Novant Health Midtown Family Medicine. He loved it so much he's set a goal to participate as a runner.

Gerald says that his wife and fellow team members helped him make lasting changes. Now he's cheering on others – something we can all do. Let's take a page from Gerald's story and give one another the encouragement we need to live the healthy lives we want.

Section 3

DNA and building with teamwork

Nurses draw and architects care, or vice versa?

In the past, architects designed hospital units and nurses cared for patients on those units. And the lines of responsibility never blurred.

Until now.

To successfully transform patient care, we also have to transform the space in which we provide care. And that's exactly what a team of professionals is doing for our patients, staff and hospitals.

When the two-floor expansion at Novant Health Huntersville Medical Center recently opened – for medical-surgical and women's health – each unit incorporated the design work from a team of staff including nurses, physicians, pharmacists, supply chain specialists, architects and other disciplines.

While teams in healthcare are not a new concept, this particular group was unique. They're redesigning our facilities based upon two key tenets: (1) patient focused; (2) caregiver driven. Yes, designing beautiful rooms and spaces is still important and so is keeping the cost of construction and renovation affordable. Caregivers, however, lead the design and focus that work on patient care and optimizing their time with patients and families.

This "caregiver as architect" model still relies heavily on the experts from our construction and real estate division, but now the clinical staff who work and care for patients on the units help shape their physical surroundings. These teams are designing prototypes that build from the ideas of others. For instance, another team is putting to use the creative work from Huntersville Medical Center to design the expansion at Novant Health Matthews Medical Center that includes the intensive care unit, oncology and the step-down unit. In addition, a design team of caregivers and other staff at Novant Health UVA Health System Prince William Medical Center in northern Virginia are incorporating the ideas from both Matthews Medical Center and Huntersville Medical Center as they build a new community hospital in Haymarket.

As a health system, we're improving how we leverage good ideas. It's essential for us to share and implement great solutions, like the work of these design teams. The following are examples of improvements made that benefit patients and clinical staff:

- Changing the shape of the room from rectangular to square, which provides more clearance around the patient for staff and equipment during emergencies.

- Decentralizing medications and supplies by locating supply cabinets between patient rooms. Staff have estimated that during a 24-hour shift, this single change eliminated 400 minutes of hunting for and gathering supplies.

- Converting from "nursing stations" to "huddle stations" where nurses, physicians, therapists and other staff discuss a patient's plan of care, in a physical setting closer to patient rooms.

- Realizing other benefits that make providing care more affordable, such as less square footage, less water usage and achieving Energy Star ratings.

We shouldn't be surprised that our patients and their families are noticing these changes. They may not articulate the slight nuances of a physical design change, but they are recognizing that their care team is spending more time with them. Thanks to everyone involved with this creative design work. It's been remarkable.

Worst storm in years brings out our best

The heaviest snowstorm to hit our footprint in a decade closed schools and many businesses but not us. We understand that healthcare comes with a 24/7 obligation to be there for our patients – even when facing snow, sleet and freezing rain. The terrible weather didn't stop us. It brought out

From every location, I heard stories about transportation challenges being met through kindness and determination.

our best. And I'm very proud of the amazing team effort you gave to overcome adversity and keep delivering on our brand promise. Thank you for your extraordinary commitment and selfless sacrifices!

I've heard many impressive reports about what happened at our acute care facilities as soon as we knew that a crippling storm was heading our way. Our advance preparations included stocking up on supplies and ensuring that we had rooms for team members who would come in early or couldn't make it home due to the storm. And those steps paid off as we ended up housing hundreds of team members when travel became extremely difficult.

I'm inspired by your willingness to make things work. I understand that it required time away from your families when they were feeling the need for you to be with them. I know that some of you didn't make it home for three days. That's difficult and led to the team members at Novant Health Kernersville Medical Center throwing a "slumber party" in the cafeteria as a way to create some fun and fellowship.

Another example of our caring and committed culture was the flexibility many of you demonstrated in stepping out of your routine and doing something different. At Novant Health Rowan Medical Center, the executive team and radiology team filled in to deliver patient meals to cover a shortage in staffing for food services. I'm also pleased to know that our public safety officers at Novant Health Presbyterian Medical Center left the grounds to help nearby stranded drivers. And plant engineering at all of our facilities had to battle the snow and ice to keep our sidewalks, parking lots and driveways accessible and safe for our patients and team members.

From every location, I heard stories about transportation challenges being met through kindness and determination. Departments coordinated carpools, using the four-wheel drive vehicles of team members to get them to work safely. When Danielle Farmer's car got stuck in the snow, Jamie and John, fellow team members from Novant Health Forsyth Medical Center, were passing by. They stopped, moved her car to a safe place and took her to the hospital with them. That's a good story, but their Forsyth Medical Center colleague's rescue effort was even better. Carrie Rogers noticed an ambulance in a ditch on the side of the road and stopped to pull it out with her truck. Unfortunately, the ambulance slid back into the ditch, so she towed it all the way to Forsyth Medical Center.

At Novant Health Clemmons Medical Center, some family members supported hungry team members by delivering groceries to the facility, which doesn't have a cafeteria yet.

With highways closed, having enough supplies was a common concern at each location. The team at the Novant Health Logistics Center responded to this challenge, staying in touch with the facilities to know what was needed and bringing in extra teams over the weekend to fully restock our medical centers. Through this effort, we're prepared to go back to our usual routine.

I'm sure there are many other great examples of how we worked as a team to make it through the storm. Please share them with me by posting your stories on the blog. I can't wait to read what you did to overcome such a huge challenge. And, once again, thank you for doing what you do best – delivering remarkable patient experiences, in every dimension, every time and even in terrible weather.

What can Navy SEALs teach Novant Health? A lot.

D elivering remarkable healthcare to people every single day is deeply rewarding. It's also one of the most demanding callings most of us will ever have. That's why I was struck recently by the ways in which lessons learned in Navy SEAL training apply to what we do here at Novant Health.

We're entering the college graduation season, and recently I viewed online the commencement address given by Admiral William McRaven at the University of Texas. The admiral told the graduates that they have the potential to change the world – if they are willing to do the tough work it takes to get there. To explain, he described his experience training to become a Navy SEAL. That training, he said, "seeks to find those students who can lead in an environment of constant stress, chaos, failure and hardships."

Every morning, before heading into a grueling day of calisthenics and drills designed to test the trainees to the limit, they were required to make their beds to absolute perfection. At the time, it seemed like a silly demand. But it required the trainees to care about detail. That's so true here at Novant Health, where accomplishing great things requires us to first be faithful in small things.

Many of the other life lessons the admiral relayed share a common theme: bravery and perseverance in the midst of daunting circumstances. The recruits had to swim in shark-infested waters and were told to be prepared to fight off a shark if it approached. They were marched into icy mud up to their necks, where they had to remain all night. The training may have seemed cruel, but it was aimed at turning the men into SEALs who could charge into the worst of danger and complete a mission.

The SEAL trainees learned quickly they would never survive alone. During boat drills in towering waves, every person in the boat was needed. If just one person stopped paddling, the crew could sink. "If you want to change the world," Admiral McRaven told his audience, "find someone to help you paddle." Such teamwork is the essence of our organization: a group of people with unique talents who, combined and leaning on one another, do extraordinary things.

Challenges test us, not just in the world of the SEALs, but in our personal lives and in the world of healthcare. Failures discourage us. But what we can accomplish in the light is determined by who we are in the dark.

I'm convinced that the team at Novant Health is changing the delivery of healthcare – and thus the lives of countless individuals and families – throughout our communities. We're doing it by faithfully performing the small, seemingly mundane tasks. We're doing it with resilience and bravery. And most of all, we're doing it together.

Critical thinking solves annoying problem

A few months ago, Amanda Lineberry, a clinical unit leader at Novant Health Forsyth Medical Center, posted a comment on my blog about the "nurse button" on the beds in her unit not working. At that time, I asked Moe Houston and Mark Webster to work on it immediately. And I was pleased to hear that the issue was quickly resolved.

Even though the fix turned out to be simple, it's worth discussing because the only way to keep the problem from happening over and over again is through teamwork and communication.

As with most of our hospital beds, those in Amanda's unit include a system that allows the patient to control the TV and room lighting and to request nursing assistance. Moe and Mark found that the beds believed to be out-of-order merely needed to have the power cord plugged in and a communication cable reconnected. This action would allow patients to send alerts to the nurses station. The connections had been lost when the beds were moved to clean the rooms or transport patients.

Shayna Johnson, charge nurse on duty at that time, rallied her team to help Moe and Mark survey the beds in the unit. They returned all of them to working status, but their effort didn't stop there. They recognized the need for process improvements on the unit or the beds would soon be disconnected again.

Nursing and clinical engineering worked together to implement a long-term solution that included adding an item to a falls prevention checklist already in use. The new item required nurses to inspect the power cord and communication cable to make sure they were properly connected. To supplement this action, detailed instructions about using the bed, including how to set the bed alarm, were printed for placement on the beds.

Clinical engineering also demonstrated how the beds work to nursing, patient transport and environmental services team members. As a result, service calls to repair the beds have declined dramatically, and we're better meeting the needs of our patients. These practices, including the falls prevention checklist, are in the process of being adopted for use across our system.

We work in a complicated environment where many specialized teams need to be "plugged in" for everything to work properly. Our best efforts occur when the appropriate teams are involved in clarifying an issue, conducting the discovery process, envisioning and co-constructing solutions, and then delivering and sustaining them. Through effective teamwork and communication, we enhance buy-in and stimulate vision and creativity.

I applaud the work of the teams that applied their critical thinking skills to resolve the bed challenge. And I encourage all of you to think of this example when facing situations where changes are needed. It takes committed team members working together and communicating clearly to deliver remarkable patient experiences.

Diversity is part of our DNA

I'm always pleased when Novant Health receives recognition for being one of the best in the healthcare industry. When it involves our mission, vision or values, I'm especially excited. That's what happened recently. DiversityInc ranked us as third in the nation among hospitals and health systems for our diversity programs and achievements.

We're in excellent company as the top 10 included the Cleveland Clinic in fifth and Mayo Clinic in eighth. These rankings come from a valued source as DiversityInc leads the nation in advancing and recognizing excellence in diversity management.

It took a lot of hard work by our diversity councils and business resource groups to earn this honor. For many years, they have been helping us build and enhance the diversity programs that are setting us apart as a leader. They also contributed to the completion of a 300-question survey that DiversityInc used to measure our talent pipeline, equitable talent development, CEO/leadership commitment and supplier diversity.

Diversity is in our values along with compassion, personal excellence and teamwork because it permeates our organization and is part of the very fiber of who we are and why we exist. Diversity and its partner – inclusion – are integrated into Novant Health's DNA.

As we look forward, our goals include leveraging diversity and inclusion to deliver remarkable patient experiences, allowing all team members to contribute to their full potential and ensuring all stakeholders feel welcomed and respected. We can only achieve our mission when we value each person and treat them the way they want to be treated.

To make this happen, every team member must be involved. That includes me. I contribute by chairing the Novant Health executive diversity council and meeting periodically with our seven business resource groups that are focused on addressing the unique needs of a wide range of population segments – African-American, Hispanic, women, lesbian/gay/bisexual/transgender, Asian, generational, and veterans and individuals with disabilities. These groups help us see what we can do to make Novant Health even more diverse and inclusive than it already is.

You can also help support our diversity vision by learning more about how to best meet the diverse needs of our patients and communities. A new manual about cultural and religious considerations will soon be available on I-Connect and promoted to all team members. I encourage you to review the manual and apply it to your work in patient care. It's also a great resource for building stronger relations with other team members. Each person is different as he or she is shaped by unique life experiences. The manual is intended to enhance relationships with our patients and their families by providing improved understanding of how they would like to be treated. At the same time, it isn't a blueprint. You should still respectfully ask patients if there is any information you need to know about their beliefs, practices and preferences.

Congratulations to our diversity team and everyone who supported the effort to earn this recognition not merely by participating in the survey process but through daily efforts to ensure that diversity is part of who we are. It's a critical part of the remarkable patient experience and essential to being a great place to work. I hope all of you understand why we value diversity as well as inclusion and will make them part of who you are daily.

It's our Super Bowl moment – the electronic health record

I f you're a football fan like me, you probably were among the more than 100 million Americans who watched at least part of the Super Bowl yesterday. For some, it's just a reason to party. But I find it intriguing to see which team best uses its talent to win.

The path to this year's Super Bowl demonstrated the value of communication in having a championship team. When sending in plays from the sidelines or changing them at the line of scrimmage in a noisy stadium, the teams found ways to communicate clearly with all the players involved and to do it quickly.

We also face the need to share information with team members in a timely manner across all aspects of our organization. For us, the goal isn't winning a trophy. It's providing a remarkable patient experience – helping someone get better and stay healthy.

To make that happen for thousands of people daily, our strategic plan that I've been reviewing over the past two weeks includes the successful implementation of Dimensions, our fully integrated electronic health record.

Empower. That's the word we use to describe what Dimensions is doing for us. It's empowering each of us to deliver remarkable patient experiences by making timely, accurate information readily accessible. Our guiding principles in designing Dimensions include being centered on patients and focused on safety and quality. They also envision information flowing seamlessly across our organization to help our providers make timely and correct decisions for their patients.

Last year, we completed the rollout of Dimensions Ambulatory in our medical group clinics. Meaningful use of this new technology has been achieved at nearly all of our clinics and has improved the interaction between patients, staff and physicians. Novant Health has become a national leader in the adoption of MyChart, improving both engagement with patients and efficiency for staff and providers in our clinics.

We also launched Dimensions Acute at Novant Health

It's empowering each of us to deliver remarkable patient experiences by making timely, accurate information readily accessible.

Presbyterian Medical Center in 2013 and received positive patient feedback within days. The use of Dimensions immediately enhanced conversations among physicians and nurses about a patient's condition. And physicians' discussions with patients about their treatment became more effective as a computer screen is shared for reviewing data together. We have already seen the benefits of a single patient record as patients have transitioned from care at the hospital to an office without the need for faxes or phone calls to request records. I'm excited that we're using Dimensions to better engage patients as partners in caring for their health.

This year, we will finish the rollout of Dimensions Acute across the remainder of the greater Charlotte market and for most of the greater Winston-Salem market. The rest of Novant Health will transition to Dimensions in 2015. We'll apply what we learned from the rollout at Presbyterian Medical Center, but every go-live is unique and requires a team effort. That's why we'll continue to use our proven change management process that has helped us deal with risks through training, follow-up and support.

Be a partner in change by being enthusiastic about transitioning to Dimensions. It's a powerful tool that enhances care and communication for our patients and ultimately helps us deliver on our vision of the remarkable patient experience.

Overused, but not here – the word "teamwork"

We went into the Dimensions wave 2 go-live last month with high expectations for a smooth and successful implementation that would involve most of our acute care facilities in the greater Winston-Salem market. The initial and ongoing reports indicate that it went even better than expected. I'm thrilled with the outcome and recognize that several factors contributed to our success, but none was more critical than having effective teamwork across our markets.

The task our team faced could have been overwhelming as it was the largest of our go-live events, but the team members stood united, trusted and relied upon one another, and proved that working together is the best way to achieve success. The results and how we achieved them demonstrated that teamwork is truly being embraced as a Novant Health value.

It took the commitment of many individuals to make this group effort work. The team included more than 6,500 end users on Dimensions Acute who were trained in a six-week period before the go-live. These end users received elbow-to-elbow support from our wave 2 super users, vendor partner Leidos and consulting partner Epic.

Valuable assistance was also provided by Novant Health team members from the greater Charlotte market. As participants in the wave 0 and wave 1 go-live, these team members understood that it would be hard work, but they didn't hesitate to take on the challenge again because they wanted to support their colleagues facing wave 2. These wave 0 and wave 1 veterans tapped into another Novant Health value – compassion – and used it as motivation to jump in and help. They knew from hands-on experience how difficult the implementation would be and wanted to be there to make it easier for their Novant Health "family members." In this way, compassion brought hearts, not just minds and hands, into the teamwork.

Having documented and applied many lessons learned from our past efforts, we found that the number of issues needing to be fixed during the wave 2 go-live was much lower compared to the first two waves. And we had incorporated some of these lessons into our training program, resulting in fewer user errors in wave 2 compared to the previous waves. Patients commented that they were treated with kindness and courtesy during their hospital stay even though the implementation was underway. Reports from a financial perspective are also encouraging.

The immediate benefit of the go-live is that another large part of our organization has gained the ability to see real-time patient information at the bedside while building authentic, personalized relationships with patients. With each implementation, Dimensions technology moves us toward a more standardized and efficient approach to patient care delivery. When completed, information will be accessible to our caregivers regardless of where the patient enters our system.

I applaud the teamwork, compassion and commitment to the Dimensions guiding principles that made wave 2 our best go-live yet despite it being our biggest project to manage. Thank you for working as a team across markets and finding solutions to issues that meet the needs of our entire system. My key takeaway from wave 2 is that our culture positions us to continue producing excellent results that will be the envy of the healthcare industry. That's a great place to be. Let's keep it going by staying true to our mission, vision and values.

What trees taught me about teamwork

One Saturday earlier this year, I decided it was time to clear some trees on the land I own in Forsyth County. It was a beautiful day to go outside, get some fresh air and work up a sweat. I couldn't wait to fire up the tractor and start working.

My plan was to pile the dead trees in a corner of the property. Maybe they would become firewood or, more likely, a home for black rat snakes. This chore was going to take a few hours, but I had all day, plus I was looking forward to being productive.

Everything was going well as I worked several hours piling up trees, but then a large sharp branch from a pine came crashing down. It harpooned the side of the tractor, bringing the drive gear to a halt. "No problem," I told myself. I was confident I could get it out by myself. I spent quite a bit of time trying to remove the limb, but I was going nowhere. The more I tried, the greater the grip of the gears seemed to be.

It took me a while, but I eventually realized this was not a one-person job. I was going to need assistance. Lucky for me, a friend was able to come down and the two of us managed to pull out the branch. We then investigated how much damage had been done. And you know what? He was more than happy to help me out, just like I would have helped him out if he had been in my situation.

It made me stop and think about how many times I've shared in this blog how much stronger we are working together as a team. On this particular day, I was enjoying working outside in the cool breeze by myself and was proud I was accomplishing this task on my own. However, when trouble arose, I needed to call a friend for assistance.

So why is it some of us avoid asking for help or guidance? I know we all would be happy to lend a helping hand when a colleague needs it. Sometimes, all we need to do is ask: Can you help me with this? Do you know how to do that? Do you have any advice before I start this task? These are questions many of us have, whether you work in the medical center, the outpatient clinic or the revenue cycle center. Likewise, if you see someone struggling at work, find a way to offer some guidance.

As a team, we know we work more efficiently together. Yet there are still times when some of us wait until things aren't going well before we'll speak up. My reminder from my tractor dilemma is that we shouldn't be afraid to ask for help. Don't grind your gears if you don't have to. No one has to go it alone at Novant Health – we're all in this together.

Compassion and creativity solve ER mystery

It's always inspiring when we hear of team members being resourceful in order to make our patients' experiences better. I want to share a story from Novant Health Rowan Medical Center that illustrates the good we can do when we act with compassion and creativity.

Being able to identify someone with an iris scan provides an extra layer of security against medical identity theft.

When Stacey, a patient access specialist, arrived for her shift at Rowan Medical Center's emergency room on a recent evening, she faced a puzzling situation. A patient had arrived by ambulance without any identification. The middle-aged woman had been walking up to houses in a neighborhood, knocking on doors. When the ambulance crew found her, she was wandering in a nearby field. She could speak, but she didn't know her name, address or anything at all about herself. It's a scary situation for a person to be in – not to remember where you live or even who you are.

Rowan Medical Center nurses had already contacted police departments to see if the woman had been reported missing, but had no luck.

Stacey suggested the team try the emergency room's biometric camera, which scans a patient's eyes. As most of you know, Novant Health has invested in biometric patient identification technology as a way to enhance patient safety and privacy.

When patients enroll in this program, we capture images of their faces and irises. That information is linked to patients' names and records. Being able to identify someone with an iris scan provides an extra layer of security against medical identity theft. In the case of Rowan Medical Center's "Jane Doe," it did even more.

"We wheeled her out front and did an eye scan," Stacey said. "Bingo! We now had the identity of our 'Jane Doe.' Thankfully, somebody had previously enrolled her in the program."

Stacey and the Rowan Medical Center emergency room team creatively solved a problem and helped our patient on her way, not only to appropriate medical care, but back to herself and her family. Their use of our leading-edge technology – both by enrolling the patient earlier in the biometric system and by using the system on the woman's visit that night to the emergency room – helped the patient get the compassionate care she deserved.

Thank you, Stacey and the entire Rowan Medical Center emergency room team, for being resourceful and persistent in providing such a remarkable patient experience.

Creating a playbook, for football and healthcare

At Novant Health, we've been recognized as a leader in improving the quality of healthcare many times. To consistently deliver the right care, we need teamwork and discipline. They're at the center of everything we do for our patients. And as I've watched football this season, I realize that there are a lot of parallels between the teamwork and discipline it takes to win games and the teamwork and discipline needed to deliver quality healthcare.

If you're like me, you've enjoyed watching football this year, especially if you're a fan of our hometown teams in the Carolinas or Washington, D.C. Both teams played well throughout the year, earning them a spot in the playoffs.

To play and win at this level, a team needs every player contributing in a coordinated, disciplined way. In football, that means players perfect every aspect of the game – repeatedly running routes, returning punts, kicking field goals. In the offensive playbook, every play is choreographed and each player given an assignment. When a play doesn't work, the team – both players and coaches – makes adjustments until it does.

Healthcare has a playbook as well. We have policies and protocols for wearing personal protective equipment and prescribing the correct antibiotics. Red rules ensure we treat the right patient. To prevent infections, all of us must follow appropriate hand hygiene procedures. Many of our teams – environmental, surgical and others – follow a checklist because highly reliable, safe patient care requires well-defined steps and attention to the details.

This type of discipline leads to successful, high-performing teams. On the football field, it leads to winning seasons and playoff berths. For us, success means that patients receive the right care and medications and that our infection rates are low. It means we are delivering on our vision of the remarkable patient experience. That's a team I'm honored to be a part of. Thank you for your teamwork and discipline.

I'm also proud of the Carolina Panthers this year. Whether they win or lose the Super Bowl, the 2015 season has definitely been one to remember.

Here's your challenge – pay it forward

When you're working hard, giving of your time and talent, nothing feels better than to be recognized for that effort. We all want to be appreciated. I thought about that recently when I heard about one department taking time to thoughtfully say "thank you" to various teams in the organization.

As I understand it, the marketing and communications department recently delivered small tokens of gratitude and notes of thanks to a variety of teams at hospitals and clinics across the organization.

You may have been on the receiving end of their efforts. The team handed out little items such as fortune cookies (with notes that said "We're fortunate to have you") and lip balm ("You're the balm!"). As you might imagine, it's not about getting lip balm – it's about having a team member smile at you, notice you, and remind you how valuable your work is to the team and our patients. Some of the folks receiving the thanks said it was a real highlight for that day. And as we all know, when we bless someone with kindness, we feel pretty good ourselves.

As I look around me at the people who serve at Novant

Health, what I see is a determination to pull together as a team to do the right thing for patients and one another, every day, under every possible circumstance. Whether you work directly with patients or in a role that enables care to happen, remember that your contributions count.

And now I am challenging you and your team to find a way to say "thank you" to others here at Novant Health; let's create a pay-it-forward movement across the organization. I'd love to hear more about how you "pay it forward" and see photos that capture how you thank your colleagues. I've asked our corporate communications team to be on point for receiving them and sharing them on I-Connect and in Team Connect.

Let's all look for opportunities to thank team members – to express appreciation for a positive spirit, a creative solution, a willingness to help. Examples of this kind of resiliency and teamwork are all around us. Thank you! I appreciate all you do!

Our vision and team of 26,000

As I mentioned last week, we simplified the message in our vision statement about who delivers the most remarkable patient experience. Instead of including a specific reference to physician partners, the "we" in the vision statement is now defined as "the Novant Health team."

We, **the Novant Health team**, will deliver the most remarkable patient experience in every dimension, every time.

When the vision was first created, we needed to make it clear that physician partners were included. Now, they are such an integral part of our team that we no longer need to make that distinction. This change reinforces the understanding that we've always had about every member of the team being an important link in how we serve our patients and their families. This change reflects how far Novant Health has come over the past several years.

And the vision requires that our leaders create an engaged

environment that makes all people who work here feel that they are part of a special team. Everyone is valued. Another change announced in October, we now say "team member" when talking about each other instead of using the words "employee" or "staff." We also work side by side every day with individuals who are not officially employed by Novant Health. Independent medical staff members, volunteers, vendors and independent contractors all fall into that category. Yet we couldn't do our jobs without them, so we consider them team members, too.

It takes teamwork to bring the vision of delivering the remarkable patient experience to life. How well we deliver our vision as a team starts at the individual level, with the volunteer who greets patients in the waiting room, the imaging tech who helps with their MRI and the hematologist who diagnoses leukemia in its early stage. As each of us commits to this vision, it becomes more than 26,000 of us working together. We have become one unified team.

Teams embrace the "best work on the planet"

That's a bold claim. A physician leader used that phrase to describe all of the challenging and passionate work occurring at Novant Health to reduce unwarranted variation and adopt best practices in how we provide patient care.

Today, more clinicians are embracing this approach to improving healthcare than ever before. It wasn't too long ago in our industry's history that similar efforts were met with fierce resistance. Terms like "cookbook medicine" sprang up in conversations and journals. Early on, many clinical staff were skeptical because they felt the effort focused on economics and financial savings, which are indeed valid benefits, but not at the heart of why this strategy is so important.

However, like many major changes, acceptance grew – providers and healthcare organizations began studying why tests, treatment, medications and follow-up care varied widely among like groups of patients. And a significant factor in this positive momentum was the realization that reducing clinical variation improved the quality and safety of care.

At Novant Health, many staff devote their time and talent to reducing clinical variation in the areas of heart care, neurology, pneumonia, critical care, cancer, women's health and other specialties. Physicians, nurses, respiratory therapists, pharmacists, physical therapists and other staff work in teams to study variation. They're using knowledge, data and published evidence to improve the outcomes of our patients by establishing best practices.

For instance, one of our hospitals created a team to study why so much variability existed in the care that stroke patients received. Did good reasons exist? Was their stroke patient population different from other facilities? They concluded that their variation was unwarranted. As a result, they impressively reduced how long stroke patients remained in the hospital and improved the overall care patients received, while also reducing unnecessary readmissions. Like many similar teams, this clinical group developed a consistent, reliable approach to stroke care.

Another group of three Novant Health hospitals studied variation in the care of very ill patients on ventilator machines. Sometimes patients can develop an infection if germs enter through the ventilator tubing and into the lungs, leading to pneumonia and even death. A team determined that these infections could be greatly reduced if staff decreased the variety of methods to care for these patients and applied consistent, best practices. The results? Those three hospitals have gone more than 53 consecutive months without causing pneumonia in this

They're using knowledge, data and published evidence to improve the outcomes of our patients by establishing best practices.

vulnerable group of patients. That's a truly remarkable achievement among our nation's intensive care units and hospitals.

I don't like to overuse the term "journey," but the word does appropriately describe the work of these dedicated teams. They are spreading best practices across all Novant Health organizations because, as a healthcare system, we must share our achievements to ultimately make healthcare a remarkable experience everywhere.

Is this the "best work on the planet"? Many staff believe it is. They witness and experience patients receiving better care because of these team efforts.

Section 4

The marching brand and explaining the complex

Is $1.6 billion in savings too much?

I'm sure you've all heard this sound financial advice for yourself or your family: "Make sure you build a savings with enough money to cover at least six months of your expenses." My parents gave me this advice. This savings philosophy can be a lifesaver during a crisis or hard times.

A recent newspaper series critical of not-for-profit healthcare systems pointed out that hospitals have accumulated "billions in investments." And some have, including Novant Health and our facilities. We currently have saved $1.6 billion, which is a combination of cash savings and investments. And that savings exists for all of our facilities, for our entire health system.

The newspaper articles and some people quoted in them believe that's too much money. Here's my opinion about our savings – it's a responsible amount and every staff person and patient should feel more secure because of our savings. Now let me share some reasons that support my conclusion.

There's an accounting term called "Days Cash on Hand." Put simply, this represents the amount of money a company has saved that could be used to operate the organization during a crisis or hard times, just like the six-month recommendation for all of us in our private lives. Our $1.6 billion in savings equates to six months and 13 days, which would fund normal expenses such as payroll, benefits and supplies.

Is that amount too much? In my opinion, I think our savings should be slightly higher, meaning we need to increase it in order to become better prepared to meet a crisis and future challenges: a catastrophe such as devastation from a hurricane; dramatic changes in reimbursement for our services; and other events.

Our savings supports all of our facilities: 13 hospitals, 349 clinic locations, more than 100 outpatient centers and 5 million annual patient visits. Our savings is large, but modest in relation to the size of our organization and the extent that our patients and communities expect us to be available, in good times and in challenging times.

I'd like to point out one other fact. While we have $1.6 billion in savings, we also have $1.7 billion in debt, which is money we've borrowed for building new facilities, acquiring new technology and supporting our daily operations and community outreach. And if we did not have an adequate savings account, financial institutions wouldn't loan us funds for these important projects and services.

I realize topics like this are complicated. I also realize they may not seem as important or as relevant as our daily priorities – treating someone for cancer, helping a patient recover from a stroke or providing medical care to an uninsured family. Our financial resources, though, provide us the ability to live our mission. Our savings are not out of line as suggested by the newspaper series. And we will continue to save for our needs today, and for the future, so we can continue to bring to life the remarkable patient experience in the communities we serve.

Strong finances help build a healthy organization

When I'm talking to other healthcare organizations that are thinking about joining Novant Health, we begin the discussion with our commitment to patients as expressed in our mission, vision and values. If we align on these essential elements, we get into additional conversations. And an attention-grabber is our financial strength. It serves as a big advantage for us in attracting new partners.

This highly valued asset results from the hard work of every member of our team. In today's blog, I'll highlight one of the major contributions to our financial success that you might not be aware of. It's the role our finance team plays in issuing bonds to fund our continued growth.

I began my career in accounting, so you can understand why

*While we use bonds to fund large-scale projects,
it is important that we continue to generate cash
from our operations.*

I get excited when discussing our finances. But I hope that after reading this blog you will share my enthusiasm for this Novant Health strength.

We issue bonds that investors buy to earn the interest the bonds pay. And then we use the money from the investors to build new facilities and purchase equipment. For example, our most recent bond issue helped fund the construction of Novant Health Clemmons Medical Center and Novant Health UVA Health System Haymarket Medical Center.

Investors buy our bonds because we have a proven track record of honoring our financial obligations and they are confident that a return will be paid on their investment. Credit agencies rate all organizations that issue bonds and I'm pleased to report that we maintain an excellent investment-grade credit rating of AA-/A+. It's one of the signs that you work for a well-respected organization.

While we use bonds to fund large-scale projects, it is important that we continue to generate cash from our operations. First, we use cash to meet our operating expenses of about $10 million per day. Second, we need cash on our balance sheet to be able to borrow money at attractive rates. Third, we can invest our cash and get a higher rate of return than what it costs us to borrow money through bond issues.

We can successfully manage these complex financial transactions because our internal experts understand capital markets and have experience in handling frequent transactions. They help us leverage our flexibility in when we go to market. Having such resources is one of the advantages of being a large and growing healthcare system.

Many thanks to our finance team for making bond management a tool that helps us to continue growing and achieving our mission and vision! In particular, I applaud the work of Scott Myers, Kevin Griffin and their respective teams who lead this effort and apply their expertise to ensure we go to the market at the best possible time and have access to capital at the lowest possible cost.

I also appreciate the continued efforts of every Novant Health team member who pays attention to how we're using our funds to get the maximum benefit from them. Your efforts are like our bonds – investments in our continued growth. Keep up your great work!

We're not selling Mickey and mochas

Over the decades, many people working in healthcare have felt reluctant to think of patients as consumers. Surely we don't believe comparisons of Disney and Starbucks customer service are appropriate for a hospital or physician office? Or comparisons to Target or Wendy's?

Over the years, I've chatted with many physicians, nurses and other clinicians who admitted that comparing patients to consumers made them feel uncomfortable. They perceive that somehow the association cheapens the value of the healthcare service they provide to people, a service that is often described as one of the most personal life events that an individual experiences. And I do understand that healthcare used to exist in that environment of "we're different" from other businesses.

But I'll state the obvious: things change – our healthcare industry, the people who work here and the patients themselves. It's a new era and we're rapidly transforming. We have to understand exactly what people value in healthcare and then establish processes that will create satisfying experiences for our customers.

We continually collect information about what patients

prioritize in their healthcare experiences. Not surprisingly, we've learned that consumers have very different opinions about what they value in healthcare – largely depending on their specific health needs. For example, a mother trying to schedule an appointment for her son who is running a high fever may value fast and easy access to their physician. A 65-year-old man hospitalized for cancer treatment may place more value on long, thorough explanations about every facet of testing and treatment, in addition to his caregivers knowing that he's a rabid Tar Heel fan.

Most certainly, what people value changes as they experience healthcare across its continuum. This means we must meet our patients' unique needs, remove inconveniences from their healthcare experience and further embrace a patient-centric philosophy. In other words, we must become comfortable with patients as "consumers" or we run the risk of other healthcare organizations achieving this transformation and making us irrelevant.

I'd like to share several examples of Novant Health groups who have embraced patients as consumers.

- Lakeside Family Physicians in Huntersville has embraced a "Get to Yes" attitude when serving their patients. Tom Jenike, MD, explained that when a patient calls his office to access care, the starting point in the conversation is "yes" to the request. Then his team asks themselves, "Are there any barriers in getting to 'yes'?" This mentality is enabling them to make changes to processes that have improved their patients' experiences. For example, Lakeside bought a cell phone with a text messaging plan that allows them to text patients (with their permission) and notify them if the doctor is running late. Their patients who participate in this program greatly appreciate the personalized communication, which prevents them from spending more time in the waiting room.

- Twin City Pediatrics offers a "no flu drive-thru" clinic. They email their patients announcing the clinic and direct them to complete paperwork on their website in advance. On the day of the clinic, the pediatric staff set up a table in the office parking lot. Parents drive into the lot, pull up to the table and turn in completed paperwork for each child. Then Twin City staff open the car door, vaccinate the child (or administer the flu mist) and give them high-fives. Parents drive away happy because their family never had to step out of their vehicle.

- A few months ago, many of our imaging and breast centers rolled out same-day appointments and walk-in availability for screening mammograms as well as a guarantee for follow-up diagnostic mammograms within three days. And many Novant Health Medical Group offices open their schedules and offer extended hours to accommodate patients on weekends, evenings and holidays.

These are just a few examples of how Novant Health staff is embracing the idea of patients as consumers and adjusting practices to add value to the experience. What are some of the changes you're marking? We should all challenge one another to identify opportunities to deliver "the remarkable."

I agree with Syed - we lead!

Today's blog is the second in my four-part series about what's happening in healthcare. Last week, I reviewed the impact of economic trends and how the engaged patient is changing care delivery. I'll now talk a little about health reform, how it has affected us, and how we are managing to remain a market leader in this challenging environment.

When it comes to game changers for our industry, nothing has made more of an impact than the Patient Protection and Affordable Care Act (ACA). This historic law requires everyone to

> *... we're fortunate that we can provide health insurance for our team in a climate where the employer trend is to reduce plans.*

officially sign up for healthcare and provides a number of ways for consumers to do so.

Along with the ACA came the promise of federal funding for Medicaid expansion, but the four states in our footprint decided not to expand eligibility, leaving billions of dollars in federal reimbursements unavailable for providers. For the next several years (up through 2022), the state and federal governments are expected to cut more than $315 billion in Medicare and Medicaid reimbursements.

On a positive note, more of the nation's uninsured are becoming insured and now have access to healthcare benefits. And 60 percent of the adults who recently enrolled in Medicaid or a private exchange insurance plan set up by the ACA were uninsured.

We also see a couple of trends among employers. In the past decade, the percent of adults (excluding senior citizens) covered by employer-sponsored insurance declined from roughly 70 percent to less than 60 percent. To put this into perspective, it means that 11.5 million people now have less financial support in seeking the healthcare they need.

At Novant Health, we're fortunate that we can provide health insurance for our team in a climate where the employer trend is to reduce plans. I'm proud that 100 percent of our full-time team members are offered healthcare coverage. The remarkable patient experience is just as important for our team as it is for our patient community.

The days of low copays and low deductibles for coverage are long gone. Today, nearly 25 percent of employers only offer consumer-directed health plans (CDHPs). These plans depend on personal healthcare accounts – basically a pretax medical savings account – to pay for medical expenses. Compared to someone with a low-deductible insurance plan, you can imagine that CDHP participants will be much more cautious about how they spend their healthcare dollars.

The same is true for about 25 percent of the consumers who have a high-deductible plan of $1,000 or more. When they seek medical treatment, it usually involves an out-of-pocket payment. Consumers now think twice before spending money that's not in their budget.

Likewise, consumers are becoming more active in their healthcare decisions. We've already seen this. Go to an out-of-network provider and it will cost you more. Use a Novant Health provider and get a more competitive rate, keeping money in your pocket. We can guarantee that our team members will receive the lowest rate by choosing a Novant Health facility. We want them to have the best value and the best quality at the best price.

With cuts and changes of this magnitude, hospitals will feel the impact on their bottom line. As Syed Saghir, one of our operations analysts, said in the comments section on my last post: We really "need to take the lead and stay ahead of the game." I totally agree, Syed, and Novant Health has been working on our game plan for a long time as we enter this new era of healthcare where the strongest will thrive. Even though we are under revenue pressure like the rest of the healthcare industry, we are well-positioned to take advantage of the situation because of our effective physician partnerships and relatively strong balance sheet.

With everyone on our team working together, I'm confident that we will continue to be a leader and will emerge from this challenging time stronger than our competitors. By staying focused on delivering the remarkable patient experience for our community along with our team members, you will be doing your part to help grow and improve the health of our communities, one person at a time.

Should we make a profit?

I t is a question that often goes unvoiced: Should we make a profit? My answer to that question: absolutely. Every not-for-profit organization needs to bring in more money than it spends annually. If it didn't, the organization could not survive and its clients and communities could no longer be served. Churches, agencies, fitness centers such as the YMCA – they all need to achieve a profit to continue to finance their future and the needs of their communities and neighborhoods. And our not-for-profit health system, hospitals and clinics operate with the same basic need. We must earn a profit.

About a month ago, several statewide newspaper articles listed highly profitable hospitals in North Carolina. The stories admonished these facilities, which are not-for-profit, for making large sums of money. Two of those hospitals, Novant Health Matthews Medical Center and Novant Health Huntersville Medical Center, were identified as being among the most financially successful in the state, with annual profits near 30 percent. The articles' conclusions, though, were severely flawed. Here's why.

First of all, our health system over the last five years collectively earned a profit of 1.9 percent (this profit is a combination of two resources: how much revenue we earn during a year compared to our expenses; and any income we have from investments and savings, which some years is a negative number). As you can tell, that percentage is much smaller than the larger percentages at our two community hospitals listed earlier. Several people have asked me how that's possible. How can two hospitals earn high profits and yet our entire health system, which is a sum of all of our facilities, earn a much smaller profit? Here are the main reasons.

Our individual hospitals, clinics and outpatient centers no longer operate as independent, stand-alone organizations, like

> *Without these funds, we couldn't keep up with technology and equipment needs, provide charity care or renovate and expand our facilities.*

many of them used to in the past. We're one company – Novant Health – and we operate as a consolidated unit, even though we have hundreds of individual components. Yes, some of our facilities are more profitable than others, but not because they charge more for their services; instead, they are busier than other facilities in our health system and that improves their financial performance.

Today, all of our facilities share resources that would cost more if we operated as stand-alone organizations. Our transition to an electronic health record is a great example of that sharing. The Dimensions electronic health record (EHR) project is also a good example of how important it is for our not-for-profit organization to earn a profit. Without these funds, we couldn't keep up with technology and equipment needs, provide charity care or renovate and expand our facilities.

So, is our 1.9 percent operating profit margin too much? Not enough? I'm confident telling you that it's a bare minimum for what we must accomplish in the years ahead. We must find new, better ways of delivering care. We must lower our expenses in order to respond to the national imperative to make healthcare more affordable. And we must involve staff in the solutions because we need everyone's ideas.

Novant Health and the hospitals and clinics that formed our system in 1997 have a proud history of being not-for-profit organizations. And yes, we must make a profit. It's essential for continuing to live our mission and to fulfill our vision of delivering a remarkable patient experience.

Why hospital pills cost more

I n recent newspaper articles, as well as during past patient inquiries, people frequently are appalled at the charges listed on their hospital bills for medications they could buy at the neighborhood pharmacy or online. For example, a recent news story contrasted a $4 hospital charge for a pill that could be purchased for 10 cents at a drugstore.

I will be the first person to admit that hospital bills are confusing. We're attempting to make them more consumer friendly. I would like to offer the following reflections, which help explain why a hospital/drugstore comparison is not apples to apples.

A drugstore must factor in its costs only to the point where the medications are handed to you over the counter. Once in your hands, the cost of administering the medications ends for the drugstore. You are then free to decide how often and how much of the drugs to take. Should you take them incorrectly, the consequences may not become evident for quite some time.

By contrast, when you are ill and hospitalized, the consequences from drugs can be immediate and severe. Administering medications must be well-timed, monitored and closely documented so that you get better quickly. You are monitored for drug complications, even for your routine medications, by highly trained clinical specialists. This occurs for a very important reason – drugs that are effective when you are well may not be as effective when you are ill. Expenses such as clinical monitoring are factored into a hospital's drug pricing. The customer in a hospital setting requires greater oversight than those served by a drugstore. We constantly study ways to reduce our costs for patients, but we will not compromise care by reducing or eliminating this level of clinical oversight.

Following are two other important points I'd like to make:

1. What patients pay for medications while hospitalized typically leads to gross misrepresentations of the economics of healthcare. Many businesses don't itemize the components of a product or service for their customers. People would have questions similar to those about hospital pill charges if a home builder listed individually priced components of their products and services, such as roofing nails. Yet we are very transparent and provide this level of pricing detail in healthcare when it's requested by any of our patients.

2. For most of our hospital overnight patient stays, the individual prices on an itemized statement have no impact on the amount of the patient's bill. Insurance companies and governmental payors such as Medicare negotiate a fixed rate for hospital admissions, which means that the patient's bill is based upon a contracted, prearranged amount. In other words, the charges for any individual item, such as a pill, on most hospital inpatient statements has no impact on what a patient is responsible to pay.

My attempt to explain this also sheds light on why the healthcare industry and insurance companies should simplify the pricing and payment of our services. The current process simply creates too much confusion.

Compensation for healthcare executives

I 've met very few individuals in my lifetime who enjoy talking publicly about their incomes. The overwhelming majority of people consider that private. And so do I.

However, in a society that today values more transparency and open discussion about issues in healthcare, I've had to become more comfortable reading about my salary and benefits in media and online. My goal with today's blog is to explain how executive compensation is established at Novant Health. I hope you find this useful.

The Novant Health board of trustees, which consists of community leaders from organizations and businesses, establishes our executive salaries and benefits. I'm not involved in determining my own compensation and benefits, nor is any Novant Health system employee or hospital executive.

Executive compensation is established by comparing Novant Health to other similar not-for-profit health systems around the country. The board hires national, independent experts who guide our trustees in establishing compensation and they rely on this benchmarking to guide the process. Novant Health establishes executive salaries in the same way it establishes salaries for all employees, by using market data and comparing our positions to similar jobs. Providing competitive compensation and benefits helps recruit and retain staff.

A significant part of executive compensation is related to achieving goals that are challenging and balanced and drive us to be an organization that focuses on improving the services we provide to our patients and communities. Our goals focus equally on the quality and safety of our healthcare, improving the patient experience, transforming to an electronic health record, and financial performance.

In addition, because we are a not-for-profit organization, our executive compensation must follow very specific checks and balances. Compensation must be considered "reasonable" and within an acceptable range compared to similar organizations. We report our executive compensation annually to the federal Internal Revenue Service.

And finally, we have become a very complex organization with 26,000 team members, annual revenues of $4.3 billion, 14 medical centers and approximately 500 locations, which include physician clinics and outpatient centers across four main states. This complexity is taken into consideration by the board when establishing executive compensation for individuals with responsibilities for the entire health system.

While discussing people's compensation may be the least favorite thing for any of us to do, I also realize that you deserve an explanation of how executive compensation is established. Thank you for delivering the remarkable patient experience and submitting great ideas on this blog.

FoodMed Regional Grocery Center

Trying to explain how hospitals are paid for their services is a daunting assignment. Few, if any, businesses are paid for their products or services in the same way as a hospital.

Several decades ago, radio personality Paul Harvey explained what it would be like if other companies were paid like hospitals. Novant Health staff has updated the comparison below, using a grocery store as the example. I hope you find this insightful.

It's your first day on the job as checkout cashier for FoodMed Regional Grocery Center. Four customers have lined up with their carts at your cash register. Here's what happens.

Customer 1 gathered $100 of groceries. She tells you that she will pay only $85. You tell your manager about this odd situation, but she frowns and informs you that the store is powerless. And because she bought lima beans and cod, you must call a jammed 1-800 number to get approval to sell her these items. (Medicaid)

Customer 2 heaps his cart full of groceries. Because he stayed in the store longer than two hours, he can take as much food as he wants to, but you can only charge him $90. Four of 10 customers pay for their groceries "by the cart," so you pray that an equal number of appetite-suppressed customers shop at your store as do hungry people to balance things out. For this same group of customers, if your store spent any money on advertising, legal fees and community education, the customers who shopped in your cereal and canned goods section can deduct these types of expenses from their final bill because they don't believe your store needs to spend money on that kind of stuff. In addition, if

Based upon these confusing payment scenarios, you can see why the healthcare industry is working to transform itself.

you allow customers to use your store phones, as a convenience for local calls, you must conduct an audit that determines what portion of your total phone bill is attributable to this nice gesture by your store. And those customers mentioned above can also deduct that telephone cost from their food bill. (Medicare)

Customer 3 also has $100 of groceries, mainly bread, milk, vegetables and other foods essential for good health. She cannot afford to pay even $5. Your store believes it's important to help those in need, so you inform her that the groceries today are free. (Uninsured with low income)

Customer 4 buys $100 of groceries. You've been instructed to charge this fourth customer $140 because the first three customers did not fully pay their bills. The customer pays you a small amount; your store must collect the remainder of the bill later, typically waiting 60 to 90 days for payment. These customers that you are overcharging are getting madder and madder, and several are refusing to make up the difference. One even launched a media campaign to put pressure on your supermarket so you would lower its prices, too. (Commercial insurance)

Based upon these confusing payment scenarios, you can see why the healthcare industry is working to transform itself. On a final note, each of the four customers described above, regardless of his or her ability to pay, deserves remarkable service from highly skilled employees and partners.

Getting lost in our brand

S everal weeks ago I blogged about the value of a health system's brand. I thoroughly enjoyed reading comments about your favorite product or company and how these brands earned your respect and loyalty – brands such as Southwest Airlines, REI, Amazon and Starbucks. I also learned about several brands I had never heard of before, such as Clarks Shoes and a beverage company called Innocent Drinks.

Your comments to that blog also contained some spirited debate about our own brand and the perceived strengths and weaknesses of it. That exchange of opinions was invaluable to me because many of you correctly pointed out that team members ultimately shape what people think of us and the attributes that compose our brand.

After a lot of research and evaluation, there's another attribute of our brand that has become very evident to me and others at Novant Health. It's fragmented. And that shouldn't surprise you. Some individuals have even suggested that our health system doesn't have an active brand in the memories of our patients and consumers. Is this heresy? Just the words of naysayers? Not at all. They're right and here's why.

The overwhelming majority of patients and consumers are familiar with the "pieces" of our organization – they're familiar with the brand that represents Prince William Hospital, Lakeside Family Physicians, Presbyterian Hospital, Winston-Salem Healthcare, just to name a few of the 400 different brands of hospitals, physician clinics and outpatient centers within our health system. In contrast, very few patients and members of the general public associate their care with "Novant Health." As a brand, it's practically invisible to many of our communities. Our health system name has been much more relevant for our staff, insurance companies and other healthcare providers who might be looking for a partner or collaborator.

We conduct a lot of formal opinion research with patients and communities, and every study draws the same conclusion: People know their local hospital or clinic, but they don't know Novant Health. This doesn't surprise me. When our health system formed in 1997, we purposefully chose a strategy to emphasize local facilities and their own personal brands and to downplay the bigger system. That decision guided us over the past 15 years. However, we're now twice as large, over four states.

That's why over the past year we've been evaluating whether or not our strategy for the past decade and a half is still the right one. Can we continue to rely upon one lone symbol, the green arch logo, to deftly imprint a health system brand into the minds of patients and communities and to make the connection between our various Novant Health locations? In today's competitive environment, I believe that subtle approach will only flounder. We must now change that strategy and choose a bolder approach.

Why does this matter? Today, a patient cared for in a Novant Health Medical Group physician office, then referred to a Novant Health imaging center, and then perhaps admitted to a Novant Health hospital might never know that all of those touch points were part of the same health system. It leads to confusion and can frustrate patients as they navigate among Novant Health providers. Our disconnected brands also confuse job applicants. In addition, other hospitals and health systems looking for a partner are often surprised to learn which organizations are part of Novant Health because of our understated approach to connecting our facilities.

We've accomplished a lot together. Our staff and facilities have improved quality to nationally recognized levels. We have significantly improved patient safety. We care for everyone who entrusts their health to us and provide charity care to those who are struggling. We are making it easier to access our services and the information patients need to get well and stay healthy. The list goes on. And we must begin building these prideful attributes into our health system brand, and I'm excited to continue sharing this strategy with you and hearing your feedback.

The marching band called brand

T hank you – each individual who shared your thoughts and ideas about Novant Health's brand during my posts earlier this year. And if you didn't comment on my blog, I still want to extend my appreciation to you for following along. It can only make us a better organization when staff takes the time to learn more about our successes and challenges.

This post follows up your comments and opinions from my last update "Getting lost in our brand." I normally wouldn't single out a specific comment, but I'll make an exception. Robert, a public safety officer at Novant Health Forsyth Medical Center, shared a metaphor about marching bands that was inspired by the movie *Drumline*. He explained a scene in the movie where a single drummer was marching to his own beat. The drum major challenged that band member, "When you're standing in a stadium of people and playing your drum, the audience doesn't just hear you – they hear the entire drumline." Robert concluded that the drum major was making a simple point – that by playing together, we should be representing one sound or, in our case, one brand. Robert, thanks for that vivid imagery and for your insight.

I'd like to use the rest of my post this week to share some feedback on other points of view made by you, my blog readers, about Novant Health's brand.

"Involve John (and Jane) Q Public." As we began to study our brand, Novant Health staff conducted a lot of research. We held focus groups of patients who had recent experiences with our hospitals, physicians and even our competitors. We conducted in-depth interviews with physicians on our medical staff and with non-affiliated doctors. We interviewed Novant Health staff, leaders and trustees. And we analyzed consumer research that contained more than 8,000 local completed opinion surveys about healthcare and brands. Most of our brand strategy will be based upon this exhaustive collection of feedback.

"**The Cost of Making a Change.**" Those of you who commented about cost are right – this is an expensive strategy to implement. And those of you who consider this as "an investment in the future of our company and in each of us as employees" are also right, in my opinion. A company without a strong unifying brand will always consist of individual band members, but not a band. And in terms of cost, the single most expensive component is typically the change in exterior signage. However, I believe that a stronger system brand will pay for itself in the long term and even help us achieve more efficiencies, both on a small and large scale. For example, new signage would contain LED lighting that lasts approximately 50,000 hours versus the 1,200 to 10,000 hours of our current models, plus there are significant savings on electricity. And as most of you know, years ago our health system began to focus on standardization – of supplies, services, clinical protocols and other processes and resources. A unifying brand can dramatically advance our efforts in standardization and create new opportunities, such as reducing the need to purchase the same product imprinted with a local brand. As we continue to plan for a unifying brand, staff is already identifying new savings with supplies, websites, patient education materials, promotions and other resources.

"**We're Like McDonald's and Starbucks?**" Yes and no. First the "no." We provide one of the most personal and intimate services that consumers will ever need, during some of the most vulnerable moments in their lives. Coffee and fast food don't share that in common with us. We will never forget that inside our organization and as we build our brand. And now the "yes" response to that question. We cannot continue to barricade ourselves behind our differences from other businesses. We must become more consumer-oriented just like other industries that have transformed. We can improve our access. We will convert our records and communication to the "e-world" that has developed around us. And we will incorporate our mission, vision and values into the care that we're transforming and into the brand we're building.

To wrap up this post, I've never taken up a musical instrument, but several of my children play the trumpet. From now on, when a marching band performs during halftime or parades down a crowded street, I will definitely think of our brand as I take in the music and sights. And thanks for all you do for our patients, communities and one another.

Big news from your healthcare plan

Sometimes we get so used to something we never expect it to change. That's been true of the continued rise in healthcare costs. As an organization, we not only provide healthcare but we also assume a significant part of the financial risk for providing healthcare benefits to our team members and their covered dependents – and climbing costs affect us all. Novant Health has been working diligently and creatively to keep care affordable, for the benefit of all.

I am pleased to report that our efforts are paying off. Last year, for the first time ever, we were able to provide care at a lower cost to the plan than we did the year before. Let that sink in a moment, because it is huge news. In 2016, we actually spent less per member per month (a figure known as PMPM) on healthcare than we did the year before – $506.51, slightly below 2015's $509.22. That has never happened before, and we are excited about it for several reasons.

First, when we are efficient with our healthcare dollars, team members get a more affordable healthcare plan. But more important, because more of our covered team members are using our Novant Health network, they are gaining the benefits of its coordinated, high-quality care and our focus on prevention.

All our work as an organization – from healthy choices in cafeterias to wellness webinars and incentives to getting preventive care – is helping team members and covered dependents get healthier. That leads to overall lower healthcare costs.

Year after year, we've worked to make sure our plan stays within or below budget, which has helped us squeeze down premium increases to team members and helped us run a well-managed plan. And we've been able to keep our increases in healthcare spending below national averages. But now we've been able to bend our own healthcare cost curve! Many ingredients went into this accomplishment. Two examples:

- We began offering diabetes supplies at no charge to those covered in our plan. Providing those lancets and test strips means our plan incurs costs; but if more people are able to control their condition, they avoid expensive hospital stays for out-of-control diabetes.

- We used analytical tools to identify covered team members and dependents at the highest risk for hospital readmission, and we targeted our high-touch healthcare planning to those patients. That result: 30-day readmission rates plunged from 13.6 percent in January 2015 to just 4.5 percent in December 2016, which saves money and, more important, means people are staying healthier.

Of course, there is still more work to do. The prescription drug portion of our costs rose last year. But our medical costs fell, and the connection may be that fewer people need medical care once they manage conditions well with their medication. And we'd still like to see our PMPM come down further.

But we have a lot to celebrate. We've bent our cost curve, and, more important, we've helped people get healthier by making healthy choices easier and by providing remarkable care. Thank you for your commitment to staying healthy!

Section 5

Love of country and celebrating remarkable people

The ability to overcome disability

I learned of a new staff member at Novant Health UVA Health System Prince William Medical Center whose story is inspiring. His accomplishment defines for me what it means to overcome personal challenges.

For a student named Pierce, his accomplishment started with an internship in a special program in which the medical center participates. Called "Project Search," the program provides internships for high school students with disabilities ages 18 to 21. Project Search formed through a partnership among businesses, education and vocational rehabilitation organizations. It's a nine-month experience that replaces a school year in the classroom for students with intellectual disabilities or autism spectrum disorders. The goal is simple but life-changing – to find competitive employment in the community for students who can put to use the skills acquired during their internship.

As one of the area's largest employers, Novant Health UVA Health System Prince William Medical Center joined the unique alliance on the basic premise that Novant Health's mission, "to improve the health of communities, one person at a time," would be brought to life by participating.

To date, four interns have transitioned from the immersion program into jobs at the medical center. Pierce, who's the most recent success story, accepted a position as a patient transporter. Like the other students, he began his journey to employment by filling out an internship application, participating in hospital orientation, interviewing with department leaders and rotating through various areas, including information technology, surgical services, emergency, food and nutrition, pharmacy, environmental services and other departments. Each location provided opportunities to develop skills that the students could hopefully transfer to jobs they'd apply for in the future. In addition, every experience allowed students to build general skills, such as communication and problem-solving.

Project Search is much more comprehensive than I've described in this post. Novant Health UVA Health System Prince William Medical Center just completed its second year of participation and will begin its third in the fall. Besides the four students that the medical center hired, other interns have leveraged their experience to land jobs elsewhere in the community. And like many community service initiatives, Project Search depends on a lot of medical center volunteers.

We all face challenges growing up and transitioning from high school, some minor, some monumental. I remember my teenage jobs, which included mowing lawns, washing cars, bagging groceries and teaching baseball, basketball, tennis and sportsmanship to children in a summer recreation program – all hard, challenging work that contributed something valuable to my early resume. By comparison, though, my development seems so routine compared to the journey of the interns at Novant Health UVA Health System Prince William Medical Center.

I'd love to hear from you about an individual you admire who overcame a challenge and inspired others.

Most importantly, congratulations to Pierce and the other interns who've joined our organization. Welcome to the Novant Health team.

Taming stroke and wild mustangs

I like sharing stories that you might not otherwise hear about. We're a large health system and often there's great inspiration in something that happens locally at one of our clinics or medical centers.

As you might remember from a past blog (Aug. 10, 2012, in the archives), I enjoy horses. I'm no horse whisperer, but close, by my own accord. That's one reason David Welborn's story caught my attention.

*He praises the staff who brought his food
trays, the nurses, physicians and countless
others who help him.*

Mr. Welborn and his wife rescue wild mustangs from out West. They live near picturesque Pilot Mountain and Hanging Rock in rural North Carolina. And while that's interesting enough, he also lauds the staff at Novant Health Forsyth Medical Center and passionately shares important information about stroke awareness with anyone who will listen.

In part of our country, wild horses are considered nuisances and unwanted competitors for livestock grazing ranges. As a result, the mustangs often starve, get shot or are captured and confined in poor conditions. The Welborns help rescue these horses, train and "gentle" them on their small farm, and find homes for them.

When Mr. Welborn recently had a stroke, his condition threatened his family's passion for these wild animals. He's quick to point out that he delayed seeking treatment, almost 12 hours, while he pondered his symptoms and their possible cause. After receiving care and treatment at Forsyth Medical Center, he's diligently participating in rehab and has overcome many but not all of the complications. Now, he also proudly acknowledges his weight loss and smoking cessation.

His story caught my attention because, quite frankly, it's difficult to miss. He manifests a bit of the "wild" exhibited in his equestrian friends, but wild in the best of meanings, referring to his enthusiasm for complimenting the remarkable care he received and advocating for stroke awareness and prevention.

Mr. Welborn has called everyone he could get hold of at the medical center and clinic to thank them for his care. He praises the staff who brought his food trays, the nurses, physicians and countless others who help him. He often describes this admiration with a lump in his throat. And like many patients, he sometimes forgets staff names, even though a lasting impression still exists, like his description of an incredible "30-year-old night shift male nurse with curly red hair."

In addition to sharing his personal accolades for staff, Mr. Welborn participates in stroke awareness TV stories and will be appearing in an upcoming news segment being filmed by Forsyth Medical Center. He's also galloped full-speed into promoting the National Stroke Association by hanging banners from his barn, raising money, wearing stroke embroidered shirts and telling everyone about the consequences of the symptoms he ignored.

I possess a lot of energy. And I'm proud to tell people that I work for our health system. But I'm skeptical that I could keep up with Mr. Welborn. He's sharing our brand story with everyone, while following his passions for rescue and awareness.

Sunshine follows Tom wherever his guitar goes

I enjoy writing this blog each week, sharing stories about what makes Novant Health unique in the healthcare industry. Some of my favorite blog posts are the ones where I share stories about our team members and physicians. I'm inspired by the people whose stories I tell because their work comes straight from the heart.

Recently, I received an email from a patient's son complimenting us on the remarkable care his mother received on the acute palliative care unit at Novant Health Forsyth Medical Center. The second paragraph of his email really struck me. It said, "I was brought to tears this morning when a volunteer with a guitar and my mother's registered nurse came in and sang 'You Are My Sunshine' to her."

With one call, I learned that this remarkable volunteer is Tom Deaton. And once I started asking questions about Tom to learn more about what he does for our patients, everyone had a story to tell.

Tom, an information technology specialist by trade, joined Forsyth Medical Center as a volunteer in 2010. He often brought his guitar and played during his shifts. Tom quickly became known for his rich, baritone voice and his guitar's warm tones. He could be heard throughout the halls of the oncology and acute palliative care units.

Five days a week, Tom visits patients at Forsyth Medical Center, taking musical requests and delivering a few moments of joy. In one room, he might sing "Love Me Tender" by Elvis and then quickly switch gears and deliver a soulful version of "Amazing Grace."

Even if a patient doesn't have a particular song in mind, Tom has an innate ability to choose what will touch a person's soul. The wife of a former patient mentioned that her husband loved country music, so he chose an old country ballad to sing. Halfway through the song, Tom noticed the wife quietly sobbing. It turns out that was her husband's favorite song and she had forgotten it until Tom started singing.

Tom's gift is so much more than just playing a guitar; he uses music to minister to those who need him. A team member shared with me a blog written by a minister who stopped by the hospital early one day to visit a church member who was nearing death. When Tom visited the patient, the minister requested "Amazing Grace." The minister noted in his blog, "Tom…reminded me in his unique way that I'm no less immune to the ups and downs of life; that I also need my spirit lifted even as I was striving to do the same for others."

The stories about Tom continue. Not only does he volunteer five days a week (or more) at Forsyth Medical Center – putting in more than 500 hours a year volunteering – he also follows many of his patients when they transfer to hospice. And families frequently ask him to sing at funerals once their loved ones have passed.

Tom's music reminds us that we have a dual purpose in healthcare. Most days, we help people recover and return to life and their typical routines; however, our ability to provide peace and comfort to patients during their final days of life is just as important.

Thank you, Tom, for sharing your gift with our patients, their family members and our staff. And thank you to the 2,300 Novant Health volunteers who give more than 200,000 hours each year in service to our patients.

From Carolina to Greece with backpack and heart

The children would gather under a tent, eager to sing the ABC song and learn English words. Isra Mohamed's class of 25 to 50 youngsters couldn't wait to come to school – even if that school was a makeshift shelter in a sprawling refugee camp.

Isra, a digital content specialist at Novant Health, had flown by plane, taken two buses and hitchhiked to spend three weeks in a place most would do anything to avoid. Motivated by compassion for refugees pouring into Greece from Syria, Afghanistan and other countries, Isra decided last year to travel on her own to help. She took with her one backpack and her fluency in Farsi, spoken by Afghans. What she discovered in the camp of more than 12,000 was that her translation skills were in desperate need – and so was her ability to empathize with others.

"I saw myself in so many of these people," Isra said. Mothers, struggling to entertain small children in the confines of a tent. Families, sitting in the rain beside their few sodden possessions. People exhausted, scared and at the mercy of forces beyond their control. "Each person was somebody's kid, somebody's mom, somebody's sister, somebody's someone," Isra said.

In addition to teaching, Isra handed out food, sunscreen and sleeping bags. One memorable day, she met a husband and wife who had escaped from Afghanistan through Iran with their young children. The woman was dangerously overdue to give birth,

We all have gifts that someone somewhere needs. Let's remember that we are given our life experiences and our skills for a reason ...

but she and her husband couldn't explain this to anyone. Isra translated for them and a doctor ordered an emergency C-section. Isra waited for hours with the woman's husband who in the end was so grateful he asked her to help name his son. Isra has stayed in touch with the family, which is still in crisis – and is working to help them further.

For Isra, the volunteering drew on deep personal experience. Her parents fled for their lives after the Soviet Union invaded Afghanistan. They escaped over mountains, carrying their baby son, and lived in refugee camps similar to the ones Isra visited. After coming to the United States, they got help from church volunteers as they resettled.

In her work at Novant Health, Isra helps tell our story online as she builds Novant Health's web pages. Being both the daughter of refugees and an experienced communicator inspired Isra to volunteer. "I feel for people who are trapped and have literally no way of communicating with anyone," she said. Communication plus compassion is a powerful combination, and it's one we use here at Novant Health to meet people where they're at.

We all have gifts that someone somewhere needs. Let's remember that we are given our life experiences and our skills for a reason, and let's pay it forward by using those gifts in the service of others. I'm proud of the way Novant Health is working to leave the world better than we found it – and so impressed that our team members are doing the same thing.

Conquering mud, hills and obstacles

I f you ever feel like you're running uphill in your effort to become healthier, consider for a moment Ann Sumner. She is running uphill. In the mud. Carrying a bike.

Ann, manager of acute therapy services at Novant Health Forsyth Medical Center, competes in cyclocross, a sport that combines the most strenuous parts of road biking and mountain biking with the challenge of an obstacle course. Ann and other cyclocross athletes race bikes on outdoor courses, often in the mud, and must leap from their bikes to hoist them up hills and over barriers.

Ann's teammates nominated her as a Novant Health healthy role model for the way she encourages and inspires colleagues and patients to live healthier lives. Yet Ann says she took to the sport of cyclocross because of a health setback – the kind that can easily derail so many of us.

A longtime dancer, Ann sustained an injury to her hip and needed surgery. Dancing postsurgery threatened to injure her other hip. It could have been a discouraging turn of events, but instead Ann began looking for a new way to stay fit. Her husband, Chancey Sumner, a physical therapist assistant at Novant Health Kernersville Medical Center, drew her into cyclocross. Soon his sport became their sport.

"I absolutely love it," Ann said of racing. "It's the hardest thing I've ever done and at the end there's such a sense of satisfaction."

Last year, Ann won the state cyclocross championship for her age category and participated in a race we hosted on the campus of Novant Health Clemmons Medical Center. And when it's not race season, she's still practicing skills such as leaping from her bike to clear a barrier and then jumping back on, or running up a muddy hill.

Novant Health is a place where people bring so much of themselves to their jobs: their talent, energy and personal passions.

And when we cheer one another on to better health, it benefits everyone. Ann's whole team enjoys talking about their off-hours fitness efforts, encouraging one another to keep going. That enthusiasm spreads to patients. When patients come for physical therapy after surgery and worry that their future fitness options are limited, Ann shares her experiences with them.

"I'm 43 now and I just started this a few years ago," she said. "You're never too old to do something you want to do."

As we help our patients toward better health, it's exciting to see so many of us practice what we preach. Let's keep up the enthusiasm – and keep charging up that hill.

"If I can do this, anyone can"

Cynthia Smart celebrated her 50th birthday by taking one very big jump – out the open door of an airplane doing a tandem sky dive. She knew then that she would celebrate her 60th doing something special, too, but this time she wanted it to last a bit longer than a few minutes.

The milestone that marked her 60th birthday ended up being the Ramblin' Rose triathlon in Winston-Salem. In August 2014, Cynthia successfully swam 225 yards in a pool, biked 8 miles and ran 2 miles, officially completing her first triathlon. Greeting her at the end were her husband, children and grandchildren, and a group of girlfriends all wearing the same T-shirt – "Go Granny Go" – to cheer her on. Being surprised with those T-shirts at the finish line was the best birthday gift she could have asked for, Cynthia said. What she didn't realize at the time was that this birthday also brought her the gift of better health. That's a gift Cynthia makes a point to share with her Novant Health colleagues as an inspiration, and that's why they nominated her to be a healthy team member role model.

"Training and exercising really gives me something to look forward to every day," said Cynthia, a thoracic oncology nurse navigator at Novant Health Derrick L. Davis Cancer Center in Winston-Salem. "I really found that I enjoyed everything about it." To get ready for the big event, Cynthia trained with a group of women, including her friend and colleague, Kelli Carpenter, a nurse practitioner at Novant Health Forsyth Medical Center. In fact, Kelli introduced Cynthia to the group's trainer, April, who Cynthia said has been instrumental in her success. April was always an inspirational motivator and, come the day of an athletic event, she "stresses the importance of completing, not competing," said Cynthia.

Cynthia's weekly exercise regimen now includes swimming before work two to four times a week and running Tuesday, Thursday and Saturday. Then, on the weekend, she tries to squeeze in a bike ride along with a 7- to 12-mile run. During the last 18 months, she also entered an open water triathlon, 5K races, a half-marathon relay with Kelli, and a half-marathon! In August, she finished her second Ramblin' Rose triathlon.

Cynthia said she doesn't want to give the impression that she's an athlete. People ask her all the time, "So you can run 13 miles?" Her answer is, "No, I have to walk part of the time, but I get it done. I don't want people to think they're going to see me on the podium accepting an award." Her reward is in the satisfaction of getting her body moving and feeling good.

When Angie Flynn, clinical operations manager at Novant Health Oncology Specialists, nominated Cynthia, she said: "Cynthia is a true inspiration to those who know and love her, and a great role model for good health. Her dedication is such an encouragement." Cynthia shows that no matter what your age or fitness level is, anyone who is willing to work hard can accomplish

... no matter what your age or fitness level is, anyone who is willing to work hard can accomplish their healthy goals.

their healthy goals. And the message she wants to share is: "If I can do this, anyone can."

Thank you, Cynthia, for this great advice and for sharing your healthy role model story.

You're probably more important than a Nobel Prize

Someone shared with me a bit of wisdom from Charles Schulz, the creator of the Peanuts comic strip. I grew up reading his newspaper comic series and watching the animated television specials with Mr. Schulz's quirky group of characters.

I'd like to pass along a bit of his wisdom because the philosophy describes all of you.

You don't have to actually answer the following questions. Just read the copy below straight through, ponder on it, and you'll get the point.

1. Name the last five Heisman trophy winners.

2. Name the last five winners of the Miss America pageant.

3. Name 10 people who have won the Nobel or Pulitzer Prize.

4. Name the last half-dozen Academy Award winners for best actor and actress.

5. Name the last decade's worth of World Series winners.

Well, how did you do? In general, I scored poorly answering those five questions. However, I think I comprehend Mr. Schulz's point – none of us remember many of the headliners of yesterday. The individuals comprising the lists above are not second-rate achievers; they're the best in their fields. But the applause dies, the awards tarnish, achievements are forgotten, and so are the accolades. Being famous doesn't secure a place for people in the minds and hearts of others.

Now I'd like you to take another quiz. Let's see how you do with this one.

1. List a few teachers who aided your journey through school.

2. Name three friends who have helped you through a difficult time.

3. Name five people who have taught you something worthwhile.

4. Think of a few people who have made you feel appreciated and special.

5. Think of five people you enjoy spending time with.

6. Name five people who've helped you or a loved one during sickness or injury.

Were those lists easier? I think you will all recognize the lesson. The people who make a real difference in our lives are not the ones with the highest credentials, the most achievements or the most awards. **They simply are the ones who care the most.**

P.S. I added question six. I hope the late Charles Schulz doesn't mind. Most people who choose a career in healthcare bring their modesty to work every day, provide remarkable care and probably don't wonder if they've made anyone's list. But as my family has used our healthcare services, we've created our own mental list of the five people who've helped us during sickness and injury. I bet each of you have a similar list. And I'm highly confident many of you headline someone else's.

From zero to living in the moment

We've been featuring stories about Novant Health team members who serve as healthy role models for their colleagues. This week I want to tell you about Nancy, who was nominated by her teammates at Novant Health Brunswick Medical Center for the way she has inspired others to embrace hope and health even in the midst of an illness.

Nancy is a customer service representative in the hospital lobby, answering phones and questions and helping patients feel comfortable. She knows how overwhelmed arriving patients can feel, because Nancy had barely started her job with Novant Health when she herself was confronted with an unexpected diagnosis: She had cancer.

Fast forward past surgery, chemotherapy and radiation – "a whirlwind" is how she described those months – and Nancy found herself in remission but deeply depleted of energy.

"I was at zero. I slept a lot," she said. "I had always been active and I really couldn't even do sedentary things I liked to do, like reading."

Nancy said to get back to a life of energy, activity and health she turned to prayer, her family and friends, and an unexpected source of inspiration: the Winter Olympics.

"I would put that on the television and it drew me into a different place," she said. "I saw healthy athletes out in the fresh air. It just made me joyful that they were joyful."

That joy was the spark, and it rekindled in Nancy a desire to return to healthy activity she had loved before her diagnosis. She reclaimed her lost energy, step by step. And now Nancy's colleagues note that she works hard "to stay healthy and embrace life" – participating in everything from yoga to biking to kayaking. On her breaks at work she even walks up and down the stairs for exercise.

"I believe so much in the mind and body connection," said Nancy. "Staying positive means always knowing that there's hope. And living in the moment is one of the most important things to me now."

Nancy brings that positive outlook and commitment to being fully present in the moment to her job at Brunswick Medical Center. "There's a lot going on in the lobby," Nancy said. "I always feel like everyone who walks in that front door has a story. I try to make eye contact, block everything out and just listen to what each person is saying to me. It seems like a good way to live life – even during an illness."

I'm impressed with Nancy's commitment to physical and mental health. It's an inspiration to her teammates – and our patients.

Mary's 100-year-old résumé

Selfless giving keeps us alive to the possibilities that life has to offer – and it can keep us young, too. I got the chance recently to meet someone who's a perfect example of that truth: Mary Hunter. Mary is a longtime volunteer at Novant Health Forsyth Medical Center. How "longtime"? Well, we were in Winston-Salem recently to celebrate Mary's 100th birthday – and she's been helping patients there for 44 of those 100 years.

There's nothing quite like talking with someone who has lived through both world wars, the Great Depression and the long sweep of history from Model T to moon landing to microchip. Mary has seen enough to have a special perspective on life. But what comes through most clearly in talking with her is her love for helping others.

Mary's job as a volunteer was to greet patients and escort them where they needed to go. Some patients came in nervous and scared, and Mary did her best to engage them in conversation. "I tried to talk to them, to make them feel comfortable," she says. "I felt like I was helping."

As she walked with patients or pushed them in wheelchairs, Mary received surprised reactions from those who learned just how long she had been serving as a volunteer. She has a ready response to anyone amazed at her years of service – or her age. "I'm not lucky, I'm blessed," she'll say.

The fact is, Mary could easily have chosen not to give back and few would have blamed her. She lost her husband far too early, at the age of 56. "I had some lonely days," she says of that time. To

She's got a word of advice for others who want to experience a full life: Find someone who needs your gifts.

fill the empty hours, Mary decided to head to the hospital and see if anyone needed her help. Not only did she make a lot of friends among team members and patients, Mary credits volunteering with keeping her active as she passes the century mark. And, she says, she enjoyed "every minute of it."

Mary officially retired from volunteering when she turned 100. She says she plans to stay in touch with her team and, meanwhile, is busy at church and still enjoying hobbies such as crossword puzzles and reading. She's got a word of advice for others who want to experience a full life: Find someone who needs your gifts. "I think you will enjoy it and you'll be helping," she says.

Thank you, Mary, for your service, and thanks to all of you at Novant Health, volunteers and team members alike, for showing the kind of selfless spirit that makes our patient care remarkable!

When love of country leads you to higher ground

Public safety officer Jameson Knight grew up in the Charlotte area, a short drive from the mountains, but he had never climbed one until the Army sent him to Afghanistan as a cavalry scout in 2008. Jameson's reconnaissance outpost sat on the Pakistani border in the Himalayas, where his unit guarded the only rocky road that went to Pakistan. During his time in the military, Jameson found his passion and his purpose in life.

Jameson, a Novant Health team member since 2012, was one of our first remarkable team members nominated on my blog. He started his career at Novant Health Presbyterian Medical Center and then moved to the administrative building at 108 Providence

Road. He also serves as co-chairman for our veterans business resource group.

While deployed, Jameson read a lot of books by Bear Grylls, the British wilderness survival adventurer, as well as Jon Krakauer's *Into Thin Air* about the 1996 Mount Everest disaster. He was intrigued, and he came home knowing he wanted to climb more mountains – preferably one with a glacier. With a childhood friend, he made a pact to tackle Mount Rainier in Washington state. Less than a month ago, they successfully made their way to the top. "In some ways, I feel like this is the last true adventure," Jameson said of his June 8 trek.

Jameson trained for more than a year, hiking Linville Gorge and Grandfather and Crowders mountains. But none of the North Carolina mountains could give him the experience of hiking through snow leading up to ice-covered slopes at higher altitudes, where he would need an ice axe and crampons (think attachable studded cleats for your boots) to successfully make the summit.

The Army provided him with an appreciation for the mountains. "The higher you get in the Himalayas, the more at peace you are," Jameson said. "The Himalayas are incredibly beautiful. Each morning that I walked out of my tent, I never got over the views. They were amazing." During his year in Afghanistan, Jameson fell in love with mountain climbing.

In addition to finding his passion, the Army helped Jameson mature. "Five years in the military really helped me develop my sense of service," he said. "I feel this obligation to be in a serving role and continue to give back." As he trained for Mount Rainier, Jameson raised just under $2,000 for the National Multiple Sclerosis Society. "I figured as long as I was climbing, it would be nice to support a worthy cause, and my mother-in-law has MS," he said.

Jameson was often the officer on duty who greeted me at the front desk when my Charlotte office was on Providence Road. We've talked many times, but I did not realize that serving his country had turned him into a mountaineer and encouraged him to serve others. I do now. Thank you for sharing, Jameson. You are a remarkable team member whom we should know.

The volunteer with a cold, wet nose

The volunteer leaned over the young patient's bed and gazed up at her with soulful brown eyes. The patient stroked the volunteer's silky ears and began to talk, unburdening herself in a way she rarely did with anyone else in the hospital.

The volunteer, Dooney, is a golden retriever, and the patient she helped at Novant Health Hemby Children's Hospital is just one of many in our system who are cheered by a visit from a four-legged therapist.

When I round at our medical centers, I sometimes encounter our canine volunteers, and I'm always so impressed by the way they enhance the experience of our patients. Dogs that range from Labradors to terriers to mixed breeds arrive for work after having completed rigorous training and certification from Therapy Dogs International as well as our own screening. We've seen firsthand what a difference a visit from a therapy dog can make for patients, their families and even our own team members.

Take Dooney, for example. When she and her owner, Sally Shannon, make their rounds at Hemby Children's Hospital and Novant Health Presbyterian Medical Center, they are greeted by a series of smiles in the hallways. Children love to pet the beautiful retriever and talk about their own animals back home. Adults, too, feel a relief from stress. A woman in the infusion center recently spent time talking with Dooney and told Sally, "You just don't know what this does for me." With another therapy dog, Brooke, Sally visited a patient in hospice. The patient had been unresponsive – until she began to stroke Brooke's head.

We now know that when some patients spend time with therapy animals, their blood pressure falls and their emotions and physical responses improve.

Jane Magariner, volunteer coordinator at Novant Health Matthews Medical Center, hears stories all the time that underscore those findings. Once, she said, a pediatric patient at Hemby Children's Hospital was experiencing very high blood pressure and a pet therapy volunteer went into the room with her dog. Afterward, she said, the child's father came out, found the volunteer and said, "I want to let you know my daughter's blood pressure went down 30 points when you were in there with the dog."

Those of us who have loved pets can probably attest to what studies show – that time spent with animals makes people feel better. That's why late last year we launched "Wagging Welcome," a program that puts a pet greeter in the hospital lobby. Team members say the program provides a warm welcome, puts people at ease, and is a hit with patients and visitors.

And what about the dogs? Well, Dooney's not a big talker, but Sally said her retriever clearly enjoys working with patients. "She'll lean in toward the patient or family member," she said. "She puts her head on their knee for them to scratch her head. She loves the attention."

Thank you to all our pet therapy volunteers, for the way you brighten patients' days and bring a little canine care to the people we serve!

What's better? Visiting the beach? Or a hospital?

I know a lot of people who vacation every year with their extended family. Grandparents, siblings, aunts, uncles and cousins all get together to unwind and catch up. Some head to the mountains to escape the heat and humidity while others rent a house at the beach.

For 20 years, one family of 10 from the Charlotte area made the annual trip to Brunswick County, but the tradition was put on hold last year when the grandfather was too ill. In fact, the gentleman, a kidney transplant patient with a number of chronic health conditions, spent all of 2015 either in the hospital or a skilled nursing facility.

So it was a big deal when this man's physician cleared him to go to Sunset Beach. It was a trip that he had looked forward to for some time. He felt good, but a recent infection meant he made the trip with a central line placed for antibiotics. On the second night, his central line dislodged while he slept. It looked like his trip was coming to an end before it had barely started, until one of his sons called Novant Health Brunswick Medical Center.

That call was placed on a Sunday, and the team at Brunswick Medical Center was able to arrange for a new line to be placed Monday morning. "It allowed my dad to continue his therapy so he could stay on the coast for the remainder of the week. It was the best news our family could get," said his son.

"I can't say enough great things about the team at Brunswick Medical Center and pulling the resources together to provide that service, including arranging for the on-call technician to come from outside the county to place the new line," said the son. "It was a lot of work to make it happen. They were fantastic."

Being able to return to the beach house meant the world to the entire family. It also meant grandpa was able to help prepare a lasagna dinner, part of their 20-year family tradition.

Brunswick Medical Center is accustomed to caring for out-of-towners and dealing with complex medical issues. The vacationers may be far from home, but they aren't far from the remarkable patient experience.

To the Brunswick Medical Center team members – Linda, Wanda and Melanie – thank you all for providing convenient care when this family needed it most – on vacation.

Two daughters and 12 gifts

When tragedy shattered Connie Sprow's world, she made an immediate, compassionate choice. Her choice didn't erase her pain, but it did allow her to slowly pick up the shards of her life and find a purpose again.

Connie, a revenue cycle advocate for Novant Health UVA Health System revenue cycle services in the Northern Virginia market, has been nominated as a remarkable team member you should know for her passionate advocacy of organ donation. It's a passion born out of deep personal experience.

Their names were Charron and Tinisha — Connie's first two daughters, who died when Charron was 3 and Tinisha was 1. Connie is quick to share their names in conversation because she doesn't want her daughters to be forgotten. And that's why, when she lost them, she said yes to donating their organs. All told, a dozen lives were touched or saved because of Connie's little girls.

"When I was approached to donate, even though I was so lost at what was happening, it was not even a second thought," Connie said. "Because they were so little they weren't able to hit those milestones — they never went to prom, they never got married, they never had children … but the 3-year-old who got one of the corneas — maybe she has a family and all of these things she gets to see she wouldn't be able to otherwise."

Connie went on to have other children and suddenly, she knew what it was like to be on the receiving end of organ donation. Her stepson, born with kidneys that couldn't function properly, couldn't live like other kids — until he received a transplant. Though he ultimately experienced organ rejection

… when she lost them, she said yes to donating their organs. All told, a dozen lives were touched or saved because of Connie's little girls.

and died, the gift of those kidneys gave him three wonderful, experience-filled years, Connie said.

Today, Connie speaks to groups about her experience as a donor mom, encouraging people to sign up as donors at the DMV and communicate that decision to their families. Connie's daughter, Nyasha, is following in her mom's footsteps. Nyasha has won seven state pageant titles and uses that platform to push for the lifesaving gift of organ donation.

That mission, Connie said, is why she's excited to be at Novant Health. She's enthusiastic about the preventive care and community screenings we provide to keep people healthy. "My hope is we reduce the number of people who actually need a transplant," she said.

Connie contributed a quilt square to an organ donation remembrance quilt that travels the country. Her square features her first daughters' names and a stitched message: "Momma misses you."

Focusing on giving the gift of life through organ donation has allowed her to live joyfully, Connie said. "I do all of this so I can continue to be Charron and Tinisha's mom," she said.

I'm thankful for team members such as Connie, who bring their compassion and calling to work with them every day.

On the most difficult days, she inspires

One of the things that impresses me about our team is how so many of you make an extra effort to connect not only with our patients, but also colleagues, using creative ways to make our teams stronger.

Someone who exemplifies that commitment to team building and connection is Carolyn Edmond, nominated as a remarkable team member you should know. Carolyn, say those who know her, will find a way to talk with you whenever you need her – a meeting, a chat over coffee, a text, a Skype session.

"Even her tone of voice is calming," said Yvonne Dixon, an employee relations consultant who nominated Carolyn. "She is friendly even under the most stressful circumstances. On the hardest of days, dealing with the hardest of challenges, her inspiration keeps me moving forward."

Carolyn, director of corporate employee relations, maintains that strong connection even though her office is in Winston-Salem, Yvonne's is in Salisbury, and the rest of the team has seats in Winston-Salem and Charlotte.

That ability to connect is key to Carolyn's success as a strong transformational leader in our evolving healthcare industry. She said the secret is effective communication about the Novant Health vision and tools for managing change.

"It's about knowing your team members, because everybody is unique in how they communicate," Carolyn said. "I know I have to adjust the way I work depending on the team member, so everyone can see the vision and prepare to execute it. That is immensely rewarding for me."

She schedules one-on-one meetings or does what she calls "pop-ins" to ask simple but valuable questions such as: "How are things going? How is your day? Is there anything I can help you with?"

But Yvonne said Carolyn teaches something more – that listening is just as vital as asking questions when you want to solve a problem or tackle a new opportunity for growth, especially in times of change.

"Carolyn is the leader that everyone should experience at least once in their professional lifespan to appreciate transformational leadership," said Yvonne. "She is intentional, trusting, passionate, liberating, resilient, effective, genuine, authentic and honest."

Thank you, Carolyn, for all that you do for our teams.

Taking a break from their lunch break

R aising children is probably one of the most rewarding as well as one of the most difficult jobs there is. My kids are grown now, but I can still remember what it was like having three under the age of 7 – usually going in three different directions. That's probably why this recent remarkable patient experience story really struck me.

Becky Revalee and Karen Robinson were eating lunch when they noticed a woman with four children sitting at a nearby table in the cafeteria at Novant Health Presbyterian Medical Center. The mom was trying to feed her baby, but the little guy was very cranky. The louder the baby cried, the more stressed the mom became, who was desperately trying to get him to take his bottle while he was lying in his stroller.

The baby was tired and wanted to be held, so he was exercising his lungs and reaching out – his way of asking his mom to pick him up. But there was no way she could do that because her arm was in a sling. And it became noticeable that she was physically and emotionally struggling.

Becky, a sonographer with Novant Health Maternal Fetal Specialists, went over to talk to the family. With the mom's permission, Becky took the three older kids through the lunch line. All got exactly what they wanted: The two oldest boys got pizza and Gatorade while the little girl wanted a hamburger.

Karen Robinson, the clinic administrator who works with Becky, also stopped by to talk to the mom. "The first words out of her mouth were, 'It's really hard being a single mom,'" Karen said. Her eyes were brimming with tears. "Yes, I know it is," Karen said. She picked up the baby and let him get comfortable. He started to quiet down. The two women then talked about their children and their roles as mothers while Karen gave the little guy his bottle in her arms.

Karen learned the mom was coming from the emergency

room where she was diagnosed with a separated shoulder. After tripping over her baby's walker, the woman drove herself to the hospital. Being a single mom, she brought her four children – roughly ages 4, 6 and 9 years old along with their 7-month-old baby brother.

Before she went home, the mom had stopped in the cafeteria to feed the baby. Exhausted and in much pain, the mom of four was incredibly grateful for the help and generosity that greeted her that day in Presbyterian Medical Center's cafeteria.

It makes me so proud to know our team members are kind and generous – willing to help others out when they are in need. Thank you, Becky and Karen, for all that you do and for being a part of the Novant Health family.

Bent, but not broken: The extraordinary power of resilience

Have you ever watched the evolution of a truly violent storm? Many of us have seen them on video, storms in which high winds snap rigid structures like telephone poles and fence posts. But often the same wind, even when it gets its teeth into a stand of trees, has a different result. The living tree will lose branches, but it will bend with the wind and, when the storm is over, bounce back.

There's a word for this phenomenon: resiliency.

The ability to rise up after we are knocked down is perhaps the single biggest determinant of our success in life. And the good news is that it's a learned skill.

There's a growing body of research that supports the ideas that anyone can develop resilience and that it is even possible to experience new, positive growth after a crisis. In fact, some of this research comes from nationally recognized work being done at our own UNC Charlotte. There, researchers coined the phrase "post-traumatic growth," which they defined as positive change that comes as a result of a traumatic event. What they and other scientists have learned is that some people, after suffering profound crisis or trauma, can recover or even come back stronger.

At Novant Health, we talk a lot about resiliency. As healthcare providers, we see firsthand the impact that resilience has on a patient's ability to respond to treatment and get better. But we also see how resilience helps us overcome both everyday setbacks in our jobs and the harder things life throws at us.

Examples of this are everywhere. Team Connect recently highlighted the story of Bettielou Small, surgical services coordinator at Novant Health Matthews Medical Center. An avid marathon runner, Bettielou set out for a short run in March 2015 and was struck by a car. Her injuries were horrible and included a shattered pelvis, broken femur, concussion and broken bones in her face. The road to recovery was long and painful – so painful that it may have been tempting to give up. "I felt like everything had been taken from me," Bettielou said about the experience. She had to learn to walk again. When she tried to run, she was so seized by pain she couldn't continue.

Let's pause there for a moment, because too often I think we can assume "resilience" is something that happens easily. It is, instead, a quality born out of suffering. It's about taking step after tiny step, and deciding that we, not our circumstances, ultimately shape our destinies.

Bettielou made those choices and walked the difficult path to health. Today she is running again – training for a marathon in March – and sharing her story of recovery to inspire others. We cheer her on, knowing that just by trying, she is already a winner.

"We all have the opportunity to get better or to get bitter," Bettielou has said, and it's so true. And in facing high winds in our own lives, we can be brittle and break, or we can bend and bounce back. I'm proud of all the team at Novant Health does to practice resilience in our own work and to model it for the patients we serve.

When the team member becomes the patient

My live blogs are a busy two hours for me as I listen to concerns and answer questions on the website. Sometimes, our team members log in to share good news. One person who commented during my last live session mentioned how Novant Health had saved her life. Naturally, I wanted to know more.

A year ago, Ashley Meade, an electronic medical record technician at Novant Health Forsyth Medical Center, went in for her routine checkup at Novant Health WomanCare in Winston-Salem. Feeling something wasn't right, she asked a lot of questions about her sudden weight gain and the changing texture of her hair and skin.

Two weeks later, she was diagnosed with polycystic ovary syndrome (PCOS), a disorder that comes with an increased risk for several diseases, including diabetes, cancer and heart disease. "As disappointing as my diagnosis was, I've learned that every person I've worked with has been kindhearted and very involved in my care," said Ashley.

She's also been incredibly impressed with how often her providers work together to make sure she's receiving the right care. The following month she started meeting with a dietitian at WomanCare and also started her quarterly appointments with an endocrinologist. She genuinely feels her caregivers are on this journey with her. When her test results post in MyChart, she usually receives a message from them, often congratulating her on her progress and asking her if she has questions.

Ashley's health has improved. She no longer has prediabetes. Her weight is down and she feels much better. "I truly feel like this team of women saved my life," she said. "If I didn't have early detection, this could be a very different story for me. With PCOS, I'll have appointments to get my health checked for the rest of my life. I feel like I have the right team to keep an eye on me."

Thank you for sharing your story, Ashley. And, for providing another remarkable patient experience, thanks to Ashley's care team: Jennifer Greenly, a registered dietitian, and Laura Ramsay, MD, both at the WomanCare clinic; and endocrinologist Kellie Faulk, MD, at Novant Health Forsyth Endocrine Consultants.

Section 6

Date night and delivering service above and beyond

It's her passion to teach robotics

As you know, our new Mark program recognizes remarkable Novant Health team members who go the extra mile to deliver on the patient experience. I'm honored to talk about them and share some of their stories in this space.

Meet Hope Clubb, one of our 2017 Mark recipients. Hope is a robotic coordinator for the Novant Health system. Her clinical, administrative and technical duties cover all of our markets that offer robotic surgeries through the da Vinci Surgical System.

In this complex role, Hope may need to rush to an operating room at a moment's notice to help with mechanical issues during a patient's robotics surgery. She also closely tracks cost data to be sure we are providing our patients these procedures at an affordable price.

Here's another interesting thing about Hope. Back in high school, she dreamed of becoming a teacher. All that changed when one of her children was born premature with a heart condition. The neonatal intensive care unit nurses cared not only for her son, but for Hope, too. That's when she felt a calling to follow a different path, into nursing. (Hope's son is now 26 and healthy, by the way.)

Hope joined Novant Health Forsyth Medical Center in 2004 as a certified nurse assistant while working her way through nursing school. After completing her training, she became an operating room nurse for five years. Working inside the OR, comforting patients before and after procedures, Hope realized she was doing the kind of compassionate, patient-focused work she loved.

"When they were asleep," Hope said, "I was the one standing in the gap for them."

Robotic surgery introduced Hope to an exciting new way of helping people. Many patients woke up in less pain following their procedures and had shorter hospital stays. She still remembers her first surgery as part of the robotics team at Novant Health Medical Park Hospital. The detailed screen images showing the inner workings of the body, the robotic arms becoming the surgeon's hands – it "completely blows your mind," she said.

Today, Hope frequently travels from her base in Winston-Salem to Virginia, Brunswick County and Charlotte. She trains teams on the technology behind the robotic system that now handles a range of procedures, from removing cancerous tumors to repairing hernias.

And as she builds up the confidence of clinicians involved in robot-assisted surgery, Hope gets to live out her childhood dream, after all.

"I wanted to be a teacher growing up. I'm fulfilling that. I enjoy it when the lightbulb goes off and they say, 'I get it. Yes! I understand what you're saying now.'"

Thank you, Hope, for your dedication to teaching and to Novant Health.

The elephant in the room

A team member recently forwarded to me some comments written by patients' parents on a Novant Health Facebook page dedicated to Novant Health Hemby Children's Hospital. Before I share a few of these comments, I want to first provide a little background.

Three environmental services team members – Darlene, Karen and Pat – decided to add a special touch to their work. They transformed the routine task of stocking a room with towels into an art form to surprise and delight pediatric patients. They learned how to twist and shape bath towels into animals and other shapes, including hound dogs, sailboats and birthday cakes. If the patients are babies, they form hearts out of the towels for the cribs.

My favorite towel animal is an elephant – the three staff

learned how to make it from a 10-year-old cancer patient. Because these staff members make a special effort to greet and interact with patients, the trio learned that this child loved art. So they challenged her to invent a towel animal. And she did. And then she taught the environmental services team how to make the elephants. What a great experience for a young patient that also diverted a little attention away from her disease and toward an artistic endeavor that lives on each time one of three ladies replicates the art for another child.

When you put yourself in the shoes of a parent or child, it's pretty easy to guess people's response to the towel animals. People shared the following comments on the Hemby Children's Hospital Facebook site:

- "When we stayed over for a few days, the animals were the first thing I noticed. It was almost like being on a cruise."
- "They are always so nice and willing to be of service anytime we have had to spend time in the hospital. Such sweet ladies."
- "We love them, too! They are always asking if we need anything in particular done. Awesome group of women!"
- "They are the best. Each time we were in the hospital they always make sure me and my girls were comfortable."
- "They are a godsend and made each day a bit brighter."
- "These ladies ROCK! They go above and beyond and they are awesome!"
- "I love towel animals, so cute. Children need all the happy they can get when sick."

Do you notice what I recognize in those comments? Parents praised the three staff for something much more meaningful than the imaginative towel animals. Yes, the towel art attracts attention and can brighten someone's day, but then the team members develop an authentic relationship with people. Some of the parents' feedback describes an angelic quality that the three ladies bring to work. It's obvious to me that they think of their jobs as much more than the important duty of cleaning rooms. They're ambassadors making a personal connection to families.

If you'd like to know a little more about these ladies and their creations, I encourage you to visit the Novant Health Hemby Children's Hospital Facebook page.

They say elephants never forget. Parents possess the same powerful memory when someone brightens their child's day, especially when that child is a pediatric patient.

Chef performs "Heimlich plus"

CPR and other lifesaving efforts occur around hospitals every day. These heroics take place inside of the ER, intensive care unit and other units, but they can also occur in hallways, clinics, lobbies and parking lots. And in cafeterias.

Darrell was beginning only his fourth week at Novant Health Rowan Medical Center. He works as a cook for our food services partner, Morrison. On one particular day, Darrell had been especially busy preparing food for special events and running back and forth from kitchen to meeting rooms to restock food. Early afternoon, he sat down in the cafeteria to catch his breath and enjoy lunch with a colleague. Ironically, he ended up helping someone else catch her breath.

An elderly cafeteria guest began to cough and she eventually stood up, which caught Darrell's attention. She then pointed to her chest and started to choke. Darrell quickly approached her to assess the problem. She couldn't answer him and her red face began turning blue.

Darrell responded calmly by asking the guest for permission to perform the Heimlich maneuver. She nodded and after three upward abdominal thrusts, a french fry jettisoned from her mouth.

From everyone's perspective, Darrell's assistance and

the extraordinary moment could have easily ended after he administered the Heimlich – he could have returned to lunch with his colleague.

Darrell continued to stay with the guest to make sure she was OK. He moved his own food over to her table and they enjoyed a meal together. Darrell suspected that she was embarrassed, plus she seemed nervous and anxious, certainly understandable given the circumstances. During their conversation, Darrell learned that she was visiting while her husband underwent surgery and recovered in the hospital. Her husband stays in a nursing home and she lives alone in the city. Their chat revealed that they both shared an interest in piano and, coincidentally, the same piano teacher. The woman even invited Darrell as a guest to her church.

Co-workers describe Darrell as humble. His work combines two passions: (1) cooking, which was influenced by his father who was a chef, and (2) working in healthcare, strongly driven by the commitment to caring for his mother who has multiple sclerosis.

A small percentage of people are given the chance during their lifetime to save a life. A much larger percentage, practically all of us, are faced with multiple opportunities to make a difference by simply sharing a personal moment, such as a cafeteria meal, with a complete stranger who might benefit from a few kinds words and brief conversation. Darrell embraced both of those opportunities.

Congratulations, Darrell. I'm glad you were in the right place at the right time.

Big help for people with little

You can easily imagine the gratitude that our patients often experience when they entrust their care to us. Parents of a premature baby. A senior citizen after knee replacement surgery. A middle-aged man whose physician helped lower his cholesterol. A lost person whom you walk to her destination.

Some of these moments are more life-changing than others, but all result in a person appreciating the skill, effort and kindness of someone else.

Two groups of people, both behind the scenes, experience gratitude that often occurs without a lot of public acknowledgment. One group consists of patients who can't afford healthcare and the other group is made up of the Novant Health financial counselors who help them. A pair of stories reflects this quiet exchange of gratitude.

A woman recovering from cancer was experiencing an exhausting challenge made even more complicated because she did not have the means to pay her bills. She struggled early on with Novant Health's financial assistance application and obtaining the required documents from her bank – not because our application is extremely complicated, but because of her weakened health. One of our financial counselors helped her through the process and even contacted the patient's bank with her permission. Our counselor helped the patient achieve peace of mind by securing approval for charity care and financial assistance from Novant Health, which lifted an emotional burden from the patient during her treatment.

In addition to helping patients access charity care, our financial counselors also assist people in qualifying for the state Medicaid program, which provides health coverage for low-income individuals and those with disabilities. In contrast with our Novant Health charity care program, where we provide services for free, we do receive some reimbursement for patients with Medicaid coverage.

Our counselor helped the patient achieve peace of mind by securing approval for charity care and financial assistance ...

In another recent situation, a Novant Health counselor was assisting a man scheduled for major orthopedic surgery. Because of his injury, the patient could no longer work unless he underwent the complicated operation. The patient also knew he couldn't pay for his care. To complicate matters, he had taken out a bank loan for $5,000 so he could pay his surgeon. After a thorough evaluation, our financial counselor helped the man qualify for Medicaid coverage. Not only was his surgery covered at Novant Health, but so were other healthcare services he required, including the surgeon's fee and rehabilitation. As a result, the patient no longer needed the bank loan.

As a not-for-profit health system, we maintain a very delicate balance at Novant Health. We offer free care to people in need, yet we also hold others responsible who can pay their bills.

I want to personally thank Novant Health's patient financial counselors who help our patients in need. These staff members work behind the scenes. They earn the gratitude of patients like the two described above. And like other Novant Health staff, they help bring to life our mission, vision and values.

High-fiving and saluting his heroes

We all bring different gifts and skills to work. Dale King's special talents almost seem divine.

I first learned about his remarkable approach to work by watching a video that's part of an interactive, online education module about Novant Health's brand.

Dale works as a parking lot attendant at Novant Health Presbyterian Medical Center. Cancer patients and their families park at his location. I stopped by one day to meet him in person and watched firsthand how he approaches his job.

To suggest that his impact on patient care is immeasurable seems like an understatement. As patients and their families drive up, you instantly notice the authentic personal relationship he's established with them. Dale high-fives and salutes his patients. Why? He explains that they're his heroes, fighting a battle just like soldiers overseas. He also volunteers to walk patients to their appointments, even holding their hands when they might need a little reassurance. No matter how inclement the weather, Dale walks out of his covered shelter to greet people. And every patient knows him by name and vice versa.

Dale also asks each patient to bring along a meaningful photo. He then sketches a portrait of them in pencil, colors the art and presents it to patients during a future visit to brighten their day. His impact on people multiplies, too, as others hear about the compassion he brings to a job that could otherwise be routine.

- A local florist heard about him and now donates roses to Dale so that he can in turn hand them out to patients.

- Students from a neighborhood school made appreciation cards for Dale and delivered them in person at the cancer center.

One patient's recovery conclusively defines Dale's impact on people's lives. When the individual finished his treatments, he explained that his days seemed incomplete now that he wouldn't see Dale anymore. The patient figured out a way to fill that gap – every day on his way to work, he stops by to see Dale and they exchange a greeting.

I encourage all of you to check out the online brand program located on NetLearning. You'll especially enjoy the video featuring a chat between Dale and one of the many patients who are eager to share how he impacts their visits to the cancer center.

Thanks to everyone who finds a way to transcend a job description and make a lasting impression on the people we serve.

Date night - in a hospital?

When a new medical center opens, there's a lot of interest in its size, state-of-the-art equipment and services provided. What really excites me are the stories of lives being improved – and especially new lives beginning.

We recently opened Novant Health UVA Health System Haymarket Medical Center to serve the diverse and growing northern Virginia community. I'm pleased to report that we've already had 30 babies born there and that number is likely to increase by tomorrow. That's one baby for every day the medical center has been open.

One of those births became an international event thanks to the assistance of our team. Through Skype, we helped the father who was in Afghanistan see the birth of his child. He will never forget that moment and the extra steps we took to make it happen.

Besides maternity care, the center provides emergency care, surgery, women's and children's services, imaging, cardiac diagnostics, interventional radiology and critical care. Many medical centers provide such services, but I'm hearing reports that the team's way of delivering those services at Novant Health UVA Health System Haymarket Medical Center is producing remarkable patient experiences and continuing to set us apart as an organization that is transforming care at the bedside.

A patient who came in through the emergency department was so impressed that he said that he "agreed to be admitted into a hospital, not a hotel." He was also very excited that his aunt was able to stay the night with him. It made him feel much more comfortable.

Our first pediatric patient was a 1-year-old who was with us on his parents' 11th anniversary. The couple had planned to go out on a date that evening for the first time since their son was born, but they now needed to stay with him at the hospital. Upon

We've received many positive comments from patients about all services being excellent and the team members being happy.

learning of this situation, the nurses in women's and children's services teamed up with dietary services to organize a "date" for them inside the hospital. The nurses set up a table with a nice cloth and had dinner brought up for the couple, while one of the nurses stayed with their son.

One patient absolutely loved her server. On the morning of the day she was being discharged, the patient was ecstatic to find out that she had the same server and said, "I'm ordering ice cream today, and I'm having a discharge party and I'm inviting you!"

We've received many positive comments from patients about all services being excellent and the team members being happy. The team's enthusiasm is visible to patients, leading one to say, "Everybody must really like working here."

Pam Smith, director of acute care services, believes a key to creating that perception is constantly modeling authentic relationships with one another so it becomes second nature to do it with our patients. It seems to be working. Keep it up!

Congratulations to Don Sedgley, Novant Health UVA Health System Haymarket Medical Center president, and all of the nearly 300 team members at the newest addition to Novant Health for a successful launch and fantastic first impression. We're glad to have you as part of our team. Welcome!

Patients value the "me" factor

I'm very excited that we're rolling out new service standards for Novant Health as I fully expect them to make a big impact in helping us deliver the remarkable patient experience. They replace standards that were introduced about 10 years ago and needed to be simplified to make them more memorable and actionable – and I strongly believe we have succeeded.

Our new service standards define what remarkable means at our human point of contact. They're listed below with an action statement that helps identify how we apply them:

- Know me – I will be fully present and attentive when I am with you.

- Respect me – I will honor you as an individual.

- Care about me – I will be there for you in the way that you need.

- Delight me – I will think ahead and go the extra mile.

When you're a customer, how would you react if your experience lived up to these service standards? You'd probably become a loyal customer and even an advocate – someone who recommends that company to others. They are essential and expected behaviors for an action-oriented organization that wants to stand above the rest and provide a truly remarkable patient experience.

The new service standards were developed by a group of team members from across our system, including experts in the patient experience. They reviewed all that we know about what is important to our patients and considered feedback from many of you across the system. You wanted the standards to be easier to remember, clear about what is expected and something you could make personal. We're confident that they pass this test.

Let me give you two recent examples of our team members already applying the service standards.

- The emergency department team at Novant Health Presbyterian Medical Center demonstrated the impact of "know me" and "respect me" when helping a patient who was experiencing a lot of pain. She sent us a very positive letter about her encounter with the team on the sixth floor, which included the first nurse she met spending enough time with her to thoroughly explain what was happening and helping her calm down. And the other "wonderful" nurses, technicians, dietitians and maintenance team members were all courteous and respectful.

- Nurses at Novant Health Brunswick Medical Center applied the "care about me" and "delight me" service standards for a patient who fell and severely injured his hip shortly before he was supposed to walk his daughter down the aisle at her wedding. Using an iPod and a laptop, the team made it possible for this patient to still be "present" at the ceremony despite being in a hospital bed.

Thank you for providing such unforgettable experiences to our patients. I'm sure there are many more examples that I could share now and that I'll be receiving more reports in the future about your great service.

Look for additional information about the new service standards to be shared with you through I-Connect and other ways of communicating. I ask you to memorize the standards and immediately apply them in your interactions with patients and team members. Let's hold each other accountable for modeling them daily. Do it and watch us deliver amazing results.

Dreams of Vegas, hugs and neighbors

I love to hear stories about remarkable patient experiences. I hope you do too. Here are a few that I enjoyed learning about and seeing their strong connections to our new service standards.

Katy and Angela, certified child life specialists at Novant Health Blume Pediatric Hematology and Oncology in Charlotte, help children being treated for serious illnesses with their psychosocial needs. When these children are facing or going through medical tests and procedures, Katy and Angela provide distractions and encouragement to help them better cope with their fear and discomfort. They also work with the entire family to support their needs and better equip them to help the child being treated. And they go into their patients' schools to explain what's happening to them as a way of restoring as much normalcy to the children's lives as possible.

Katy and Angela also connect families with outside support organizations to arrange special events or provide things that are important to their patients. They recently faced a challenge, though, in making that happen for a 20-year-old patient being treated for cancer. Due to his age, he didn't qualify for donations from these programs designed for younger patients. That didn't stop Katy and Angela from trying to fulfill their patient's wish and they persuaded Dream on 3 to make an exception.

Their persistence resulted in an unforgettable event for the patient. He flew to Las Vegas where he was introduced at a show featuring his hero – actor and martial artist Chuck Norris. The patient had a photo taken with Mr. Norris that our team turned into a T-shirt for the patient to help him celebrate the memorable day.

Brenda, certified medical assistant at Novant Health Blue Ridge Medical Associates in Winston-Salem, excels at comforting patients and demonstrating that she truly cares about them. Her responsibilities include performing urodynamic tests to help determine if patients need surgery or medication to treat bladder issues, which often leads to them feeling anxious. By listening carefully to patients' concerns and clarifying what's happening in terms they can understand, Brenda builds close relationships with them.

When Brenda reassured a patient by saying "I'm here for you," the patient expressed her wish that Brenda would be present for her surgery at Novant Health Forsyth Medical Center. Even though the surgery was scheduled for her day off and was not something she would usually attend, Brenda said, "Of course." And she kept her promise, sitting in the waiting room with the patient's family during the surgery. The surgeon, Deidre Bland, MD, took Brenda to see the patient before surgery. They hugged and the patient told Brenda how happy she was to have her there.

The surgery went well. Brenda later called the patient at home to check on her. Brenda goes the extra mile to delight her patients because, in her words, "my heart tells me what to do. I love my patients."

Ankita Patel, doctor of osteopathic medicine at Novant Health Meadowlark Pediatrics in Winston-Salem, recently treated an infant who had stopped breathing and was carried into the clinic by her mother. Dr. Patel revived the baby and then spent time getting to know the mother. Dr. Patel learned that the mother had recently moved from the Middle East and lacked a support network of friends and family in the United States.

The mother came to the clinic for help because she lived in a nearby apartment complex and could get there on foot – which she did by running with her baby across the large parking lot between her home and the clinic. In line with the customs of her home country, she had tightly wrapped her baby in a blanket that Dr. Patel explained was making the infant too hot. Dr. Patel also introduced the mother to the 911 emergency number and how to use it. And she showed her how to perform CPR on an infant.

When going for a walk, she often stops by to say hello to the team. She has found Novant Health to be a friendly and safe haven in her new neighborhood.

The mother has formed a connection with Dr. Patel and the other members of the clinic. When going for a walk, she often stops by to say hello to the team. She has found Novant Health to be a friendly and safe haven in her new neighborhood.

These stories encourage me that our new service standards are already part of our patient-focused culture. They are great examples of "know me, respect me, care about me and delight me." A common thread in the three stories is that remarkable patient experiences resulted from our team members doing something special to exceed expectations and truly delight our patients. All of us must be willing to go the extra mile for our patients and one another.

The princess and the man who found a village

I've spent most of this year detailing our seven strategic imperatives laying out our future plans. It's now time to talk about why we make these plans – to better serve our patients. As you know, nothing thrills me more than hearing remarkable patient experience stories. This week I want to share two stories from our Northern Virginia market.

Jennifer, who works in labor and delivery at Novant Health UVA Health System Haymarket Medical Center, saw firsthand how heartbroken a big sister was because her mom, who had just delivered a baby girl, wasn't going to be discharged in time to celebrate her fifth birthday. Jennifer promptly set out to fix the situation. After talking to the family, Jennifer knew the little girl loved princesses. With a party theme in hand, Jennifer made a quick trip to the store. When the little girl walked into her mom's hospital room on her big day, she was treated to a birthday party complete with a princess cake, crown, magic wand and her favorite meal, macaroni and cheese, made especially for her by the food services team. The birthday girl was all smiles when the care team came in to sing "Happy Birthday."

The second example of team members going the extra mile took place recently at Novant Health UVA Health System Prince William Medical Center.

An elderly gentleman received care and, because he was homeless, the care team was able to locate temporary housing for him. Once placed, he needed ongoing medical care but could not pay. Maggie, the office manager for Novant Health Bristow Run Family Medicine, was contacted and asked if a doctor on staff could care for the individual. Her answer: "Absolutely. We'll do whatever is needed for him." The team members soon learned the patient had few clothes and, within 24 hours, closets had been emptied of pants, polos and jackets for a person in need. In a matter of a week or two, our patient went from being homeless to having a bedroom, a closet full of clothes and access to healthcare.

Thank you Jennifer, Maggie and all of the team members at Bristow Run Family Medicine for going above and beyond to deliver on our promise of providing a remarkable patient experience. Hearing these stories makes me proud and very grateful for the dedicated team we have at Novant Health. I'll be visiting Virginia for our next board meeting Thursday and I look forward to hearing more stories like these.

Canadian landing and the great suspicion

I shared some remarkable patient experience stories with you a couple of weeks ago. These are so much fun that I'm ready to share more. This week they come from Novant Health Brunswick Medical Center.

Last fall, a Canadian military serviceman received care at Brunswick Medical Center after he became seriously ill during military exercises being carried out in the middle of the Atlantic Ocean. The physician onboard decided the sailor needed to be airlifted to the nearest hospital. Jordan, the hospital administrator in charge that day, took the call and mobilized the team at

Brunswick Medical Center.

This was going to be the first time a foreign military aircraft had landed at the medical center's helipad. To prepare quickly, Jordan worked closely with Russell, a public safety officer, and Louis, a communication technician, who provided valuable insight, starting with the correct latitude and longitude coordinates needed for the pilot to land. Russell and Louis were very familiar with what needed to be done because both are private pilots, with Louis having served as a helicopter flight engineer during the Vietnam War.

Once on the ground, the ill sailor was admitted to Brunswick Medical Center. Russell then made sure the young man's colleague who accompanied him had a hotel room, hot meals and transportation during his three-day stay. He also arranged to have their passports officially cleared through the closest U.S. Customs office so they could fly directly home. Since the encounter last fall, a long-distance relationship has emerged and Russell and Louis suspect they will be lifelong friends with the Canadians they helped.

My second story is a great example of someone excelling in performing our service standards.

All of our hospitals have safety attendants who are available to stay with high-risk patients. Their job is to provide one-on-one care, which can be for patients who are at risk for a fall or psychiatric patients who need constant supervision. Safety attendants typically work eight- or 12-hour night shifts. These positions often are filled by young adults as well as retirees who may still want to work.

Last year, Greg, a safety attendant at Brunswick Medical Center, suspected his patient was having a stroke. He always keeps a close eye on the monitors in the patients' rooms and noticed this patient's blood pressure was extremely high. It was obvious to him that something wasn't right. Greg summoned the care team and his suspicion was confirmed. His fast action undoubtedly helped this patient avoid an even more serious health situation. Greg's story illustrates how safety attendants know their patients and are tremendous contributors to the Novant Health team, helping us provide quality care for those who need round-the-clock supervision.

Thank you Jordan, Russell and Louis for personally helping the Canadians, both in the air and on the ground, and for providing a remarkable patient experience. And thank you, Greg, for knowing your patient and anticipating this individual's need for urgent stroke care. Once again, I'm proud and grateful for the dedicated team we have at Novant Health.

Mrs. Z and her four-leaf clover

I regularly round and this is often when I learn about remarkable patient experiences. That was the case in October when I visited the medical-surgical intensive care unit (ICU) at Novant Health Forsyth Medical Center and talked with Christina Cassidy, a nurse manager on the unit, who shared the story of Mr. Z with me.

Mr. Z's heart failure had kept him in the ICU for almost a month. When patients are hospitalized for a long time, care team members get to know them well. This gentleman "was very sweet and very much in love with his wife, who sat by his bedside every day helping him with whatever he needed," Christina said. They had been happily married for more than 40 years and had no children. They just had each other.

Early in his stay, Mr. Z's heart had stopped, but he improved and was eventually transferred out of critical care. Then after he coded a second time, he returned to the ICU. His condition continued to worsen.

The care team knew Mr. Z loved everything about fall: the turning leaves, the cooler temps and the car trips with his wife to fall festivals. "We kept saying, 'We need to get you better so you

She wanted a keepsake, knowing this moment
would be her last time outside with her husband.

can get out of here and enjoy the weather,'" Christina said. Mr. Z, however, didn't agree. He was ready to go to palliative care.

As the ICU team prepared him for the transfer, Christina told Mr. Z and his wife that they would stop outside. Shana, an ICU nurse, and Sharon, in critical care, helped. All three were working fast because the heavy rains from Hurricane Joaquin were moving in. On their way outside, they had to maneuver a steep ramp; and to do it safely, two public safety officers, Geoffrey and Jon, jumped in to help.

They parked Mr. Z's bed next to a grassy area by a group of trees, and the couple spent 45 minutes laughing, smiling and crying. As they got ready to come in, Mrs. Z started looking in the grass as if she had lost something. When Christina asked if she could help, Mrs. Z said she was looking for a four-leaf clover. She wanted a keepsake, knowing this moment would be her last time outside with her husband. Christina thought to herself: "God, if there is ever a time to find a four-leaf clover, now's the time." Much to her amazement, the first thing she saw when she looked down was a four-leaf clover. Now Mrs. Z was ready to go in.

The rains from Hurricane Joaquin started at 7 that evening and Mr. Z passed peacefully at 2 a.m. Christina was surprised at how soon he died after entering palliative care. "But he was ready," she said.

Mr. Z isn't the first patient the med-surg care team took outside. "We do it regularly," Christina said. Patients in med-surg ICU are seriously ill and cared for with the goal of getting them healthy enough to return home. But some, like Mr. Z, do not go home. Then our care teams do everything they can to comfort these families during this difficult time, and they do it with compassion and kindness. For our patients who experience it, it can be unforgettable, much like finding a four-leaf clover.

Thank you to Christina, Shana, Sharon, the entire med-surg ICU team at Forsyth Medical Center and public safety officers Geoffrey and Jon for once again delivering a remarkable patient experience.

The bus ticket and spouse with no place to go

At Novant Health, we realize caring for the family is often an integral part of caring for the patient.

Jeanlynn King, a case manager at Novant Health Brunswick Medical Center, provides the type of care that isn't always documented in the electronic health record. Two recent cases had her reuniting families. She helped a patient buy a bus ticket to Wisconsin where his family lived, and she also arranged a surprise anniversary party for a hospitalized couple – he was in hospice care while his wife was a patient on another floor.

Looking after the family members of a patient often requires special attention. That was the case when Jeanlynn sat down with an older gentleman who had chronic obstructive pulmonary disease and was in respiratory distress. He had been hospitalized for a couple of days and was getting worse. He really needed to be put on an acute-level oxygen machine but was refusing care, insisting he didn't need it. He was anxious and very defensive.

His wife had not left his bedside, and it soon became apparent that she had advanced dementia. Jeanlynn, who frequently works on challenging cases, had a heart-to-heart conversation with the patient. The couple had retired to eastern North Carolina 15 years ago and had thoroughly enjoyed their new beach life. But the last few years, he had watched his wife's dementia worsen. He was her sole caretaker. He was struggling with the fact that there was no one else to help him, and she had no place to go. Both the patient and Jeanlynn knew his wife needed constant care.

Jeanlynn knew she needed to find a safe place for the woman while her husband could concentrate on getting better. Jeanlynn also learned the patient held his wife's healthcare power of attorney. So with his permission, Jeanlynn started looking for a supervised place for his wife to stay. She reached out to a local skilled nursing facility and found one available bed for a dementia patient.

To get all the paperwork finalized, Jeanlynn had the facility coordinator visit the patient in the hospital to go over the arrangements. Meanwhile, Jeanlynn contacted the wife's Novant Health primary care provider who needed to document her condition. Within 24 hours, Jeanlynn had found a safe environment for his wife. Now the patient could be moved to a higher level of care where he could rest and concentrate on getting better. When the patient was discharged several days later, he joined his wife at the skilled nursing facility, where he recuperated.

Thank you, Jeanlynn, case managers and all caregivers for realizing remarkable care for some patients means also getting to know their family members and treating them with the same dignity and respect.

Finding dignity in a closetful of socks and shoes

Deborah Rochelle will always remember how her grandmother matched a beautiful brooch to her outfit every day until her health began to fail. And how unpolished a simple hospital gown – all she could manage in the nursing home – made her grandmother feel whenever someone entered the room.

"She was a very proud woman, and it embarrassed her," Deborah said. "I saw her struggle with her dignity."

So when Deborah stepped in to help a nursing home patient who was admitted to the hospital after a fall – and had no underclothes for her transfer to a rehabilitation center – she wanted to find a more permanent way to help people in similar circumstances at Novant Health Brunswick Medical Center.

"I saw the anguish this patient was in as she struggled with all that was going on," Deborah said. "Our patients come to us so vulnerable. For a person to heal, they really need to know that we care about them. Helping them in this way really does show we care."

Deborah, manager of guest services and volunteers and a remarkable team member you should know, took her concerns to the hospital's volunteer council. Council members discovered that patients who came to them during an emergency often lost their clothing. People in auto accidents might have their clothes cut off for treatment. Assault victims might need to leave clothing with police for evidence. And, as in the case that inspired Deborah's work, nursing home residents might have nothing but their hospital gowns.

In fall 2010, a volunteer committee launched the Compassionate Clothes Closet with an annual budget of $800 and a mission to ensure patients don't lose their dignity for a lack of clothing.

Since then, the budget has grown to $1,000, which volunteers use to stock the closet with clothing, underwear, shoes and socks for a variety of ages. Deborah said the team, which started with her and volunteers Elaine Eggers, Carole Loof and Martha Goff, is always on the lookout for bargains, so the closet remains full. Donations and grants from First Uniform, Brunswick Electric and a collection box in the hospital workroom also help. A patient was so thankful for the Compassionate Clothes Closet that she donated undergarments after her release.

It makes a difference that Deborah is always ready to help out, said Lea Gillie, clinical administrator at Novant Health Oceanside Family Medicine - Southport. Her mom recently arrived at the hospital entrance soaked from head to toe. She had dropped off Lea's dad for an X-ray appointment and got caught in a downpour during her walk from the parking lot.

Deborah rushed over with a warm blanket, asked her if she needed dry clothes provided from the Compassionate Clothes Closet and escorted the visitor to meet her husband. "Offering that blanket seems like a little thing, but it felt like a hug to my mom," Lea said.

Deborah said it comforts her to know her grandmother would be happy she is helping people maintain their dignity in difficult situations. We are fortunate that your compassion inspired you, Deborah.

There's no place like home

Earlier this year, a Virginia patient from Culpeper learned firsthand what our healthcare team will do to provide our patients with the type of care they want.

The 80-year-old gentleman collapsed at home and was transported by ambulance to the emergency room at Novant Health UVA Health System Culpeper Medical Center. Tests revealed he needed gallbladder surgery, so he was transferred to Novant Health UVA Health System Prince William Medical Center, where he could have minimally invasive surgery.

This patient also had several chronic medical conditions, which made taking care of him a bit more challenging. So when it was time for discharge, the medical team recommended he go to a skilled nursing facility to recuperate.

His family members weren't comfortable with that. Their father had been in a skilled nursing facility before, and they felt they could provide the best care for him at home.

The man's children asked, what would be involved if they took their dad home instead? The short answer was "a lot." But the medical team's longer response genuinely surprised the daughter. "The help we received about making the decision to come home versus going to the rehab facility was huge for us," she shared with us in an email.

"The idea of bringing my dad home was very intimidating. He's not able to walk on his own and he had a catheter, so it was very scary for us," she said. "But we wanted Dad home if we could swing it."

Zan Zaidi, MD, and Cheryl Wedel, the case worker, sat down with the family and went over the many details. "They gave us all the attention we needed in answering our questions about making the transition. They spent an incredible amount of time with us," wrote the daughter. "We had to get a hospital bed, a lift and a portable toilet delivered. We're very appreciative of them helping us set up everything. It made it a seamless transition."

The patient was discharged to recuperate at home with the help of his family and under the supervision of a home health team. The daughter later sent us an email expressing her appreciation.

Thank you, Dr. Zaidi, Cheryl and our colleagues at Novant Health UVA Health System Prince William Medical Center for spending extra time with this family to make this happen. The remarkable patient experience you provided made a difference, and this family will always remember and appreciate that.

An advocate for patients, in good times and bad

Our service standards are about making a personal connection with our patients – "know me, respect me and care about me." This month's remarkable team member you should know lives by those words every day.

As a maternal-fetal medicine specialist with Novant Health, Hytham Imseis, MD, focuses on the care of our tiniest patients

The remarkable patient experience you provided made a difference, and this family will always remember and appreciate that.

and helps parents determine treatment paths in tough situations. It certainly is daunting and delicate work on all levels, from examining detailed fetal ultrasounds to communicating with parents when they are emotionally fragile.

Dr. Imseis will tell you that, thankfully, the work is joyful on most days because the news is good.

"The most important thing I do every day is reassuring patients that their baby is healthy and doing well," said Dr. Imseis, who works out of Novant Health Maternal-Fetal Medicine offices at Novant Health Presbyterian Medical Center, Novant Health Matthews Medical Center and Cornelius. "I love it when I can alleviate fear and anxiety. In fact, that's what I spend most of my day doing."

That sentiment provides insight into what makes Dr. Imseis so effective: his empathy and his kindness. Cathy Hasty, who nominated Dr. Imseis and helps Novant Health coordinate with local faith communities, works with Dr. Imseis on the shared decisions team. The situations he encounters can be challenging – women with difficult pregnancies, multiple chronic conditions, severe pain or mental health issues.

She said she marvels at how well Dr. Imseis relates to all patients, no matter their background or the situation. He always treats people with compassion and respect, she said, and that is why she nominated him as a remarkable team member you should know.

"You're dealing with people in one of the most pivotal times in their lives," she said. "They can be facing the death or possible disability of a child. It's an emotional time, and Dr. Imseis is generous, thorough, fair and humble."

Before he has to share difficult news with a patient, Dr. Imseis said he steps back and asks himself two questions: "How would I feel if someone was giving me that news? What can I do to make this situation better?"

Then, he does what seems to come naturally to him.

"I just do my best to offer compassion, to explain things clearly and to listen to the patient's concerns," he said. "We all need each other, but in difficult times, we especially need an advocate. I try my best to be an advocate for these families."

Dr. Imseis is a remarkable example of our Novant Health values and service standards at work. Thank you for sharing your story, Dr. Imseis.

Seriously ill, but there's still time for wedding cake

Our team members have the honor and privilege to share many personal moments with our patients. Weddings aren't usually one of them, but I recently learned about one that was.

I received an email from a man who was grateful for how the team at Novant Health Rowan Medical Center went above and beyond to care for his in-laws. His father-in-law was seriously ill and hospitalized, which meant he wasn't able to make his only granddaughter's wedding. It was a difficult time for the patient and his wife, who decided to stay with her husband rather than attend the event.

Donna Salyer was the nurse taking care of this gentleman. On the day of the wedding, she asked about the beautiful dress hanging in the room – the one the patient's wife had bought for the event. She quickly heard about the couple's dilemma and learned that the family had arranged to have the videographer live-stream the ceremony for the couple. "That's when I realized we needed to do something special," said Donna. She called her husband and asked him to pick up a cake for the "reception." A makeshift reception table was then set up, complete with a tablecloth and flowers.

But first, Donna had to get the video connection working for the main event. She was struggling, so she was appreciative when another nurse, Connor, stopped by to help out.

With the video connection live, the patient and his wife were able to see the wedding and reception. Plus they had a face-to-face conversation with their granddaughter. As you can imagine, seeing their granddaughter in her wedding dress and wishing her well brought tears to their eyes. This was a moment they would cherish.

Here's what the son-in-law's email said: "I am and will always be grateful for such a highly professional nurse and staff to care for my father-in-law. The level of compassion that each of them showed over the situation was as comforting as it was appreciated.

"My family and I cannot thank these individuals (and the entire staff) enough for the level of patient care and their generosity in making a difficult situation much more personal than we could have possibly recognized," the son-in-law said.

I love emails like this. And I, too, appreciate everything Donna, Connor and the entire care team at Rowan Medical Center did to make this not only a remarkable patient experience, but also an unforgettable lifetime moment for this patient and his wife. Thank you for all that you do.

Walking, chatting, listening – basics for connecting with people

There's nothing like meeting with people face-to-face to learn about them and find out a little about what they're experiencing. Interacting with a team member or patient one-on-one can be such a powerful way to make a connection. That's one of the reasons I love rounding at our facilities.

Recently, I visited the site of the future Novant Health Mint Hill Medical Center, and I made time to round at the newly opened Novant Health Mint Hill Medical Office Building at the same location. I had a great time and met so many passionate and dedicated team members.

I spoke with Erica Berger, MD, a new pediatrician at Novant Health Lakeside Pediatrics - Mint Hill, who shared with me her appreciation for being part of a healthcare system that puts patients first. I also talked with Sheilja Patel, a Lakeside Pediatrics nurse who recently joined Novant Health from another healthcare system across the country. Sheilja spoke highly of the way we use our Dimensions electronic health record to enable seamless communication.

I was impressed with the entire team and with its focus on providing the best possible patient experience. Getting a firsthand look at our delivery of care is one of the key reasons I enjoy rounding so much. As many of you know from my days leading Novant Health Presbyterian Medical Center, I consider getting out on the floor and talking with guests, patients and team members a highlight of my job. I want to hear directly what we're doing well and where we can improve. I enjoy making connections not only with you, but with the families and individuals we serve.

And I think it's important for each of us to do the same thing. Wherever you serve at Novant Health, make it a point to walk around and chat with people – both team members and, if you're in a clinical area, patients and guests.

Rounding means asking questions and listening closely to the answers. It means connecting, in ways both small and large. That connection is at the heart of who we are as an organization, and it's the foundation for providing remarkable care. I enjoyed my visit in Mint Hill, and I look forward to meeting with many of you in future rounding visits!

Caring for body and soul

They offer prayers of celebration and thanks with moms and dads as they cradle their newborn babies. They sit beside dying patients who have no family, so that they won't die alone. They help families understand the medical information their doctors give them, so they can make the best decision for their loved ones' care. Every day, Novant Health's chaplains shepherd people through fear, joy, grief and hope – the forces that shape the human heart.

Patients come to us with physical needs, but we know they have emotional and spiritual needs, as well. As they round in our hospitals, chaplains serve patients, families and team members by "listening very deeply," said Rev. Joanne Henley, Novant Health's director of spiritual care.

"It's the most profound privilege to walk with people in their most vulnerable moments," Joanne said. This privilege is trained for intentionally. Our professional chaplains have master's degrees and extensive clinical training – a background that gives them a unique combination of pastoral care education plus training in the medical environment, fitting them for a range of roles.

Chaplains meet patients where they are, in the faith tradition that is important to them. Our chaplains have worked with family members of a dying Native American patient so they could burn incense and perform other rituals at their loved one's bedside. They have arranged for Holy Eucharist to be served to a Greek Orthodox patient. Answering team members' requests, our chaplains have had conversations about what it means to have a relationship with God. Our chaplains say that many patients ask the same core questions, such as "What is my purpose in life? How do I make sense of what is happening? And where is God in the midst of this?"

Our chaplains work with people regardless of their faith or whether they practice a religion at all. It's a job that also calls on many from the community. Not long ago, I was rounding at Novant Health Brunswick Medical Center and had the chance to visit with Joe Mazzei. Joe is one of our many volunteer chaplains who work in partnership with those on staff, generously giving of their own time to serve people in need.

I'm proud of our chaplains and the vital work they do in helping us care for the whole person. From listening deeply to comforting souls, thank you, chaplains, for all that you do.

Section 7

The iceman and drawing inspiration from family

The many lines that support the front

Nov. 11 is Veterans Day. Most of you will call, email, visit or remember someone who has served in our nation's military. And I know that some of the individuals you will honor served our country at great personal sacrifice.

My dad, Lucien, served as a supply officer in the Army. He passed away 16 years ago after a heart attack and I think of him often, especially on Veterans Day. I remember many of his stories about serving in the military. Like a lot of fathers, he was prone to harmlessly embellishing stories that might lead people to believe that his tour of duty placed him on the front lines. He wasn't consciously trying to overstate his contributions – it's what many dads do when their children listen to every word that gets spoken. His stories simply amplified his pride in serving our country and his belief that being a supply officer figuratively put him on the front lines, right next to the combat. He made the connection between his job, in a supportive role, and the soldiers close to the fight.

Throughout Novant Health around Veterans Day, we have many staff and facilities planning activities to honor veterans. Many of our hospitals sponsor community events that pay tribute to veterans and those currently serving in our military. Many staff members in our clinics and facilities make an effort to extend a simple thank you to patients or co-workers who have served our nation.

I'm personally grateful that our country sets aside a day to honor veterans. They deserve remembrance and our gratitude, including a former supply officer who is near and dear to my heart.

On a related note for this upcoming Veterans Day, I hope that every Novant Health team member who serves in a supportive role will make the same connection that my dad did. All of us serve patients, even if our jobs don't involve directly caring for patients in a clinic, on a nursing unit or in an imaging center. A strategic sourcing staff member who negotiates the price we pay for supplies *is* helping take care of patients. A web center specialist who builds one of our websites *is* supporting clinicians and helping patients recover from illness. An accountant who unravels the complicated reimbursement formulas of Medicare and Medicaid *is* contributing to the remarkable patient experience. Our information technology specialists *are* helping make healthcare safer for patients. And the list is a long one, including parking attendants, engineers, administrative specialists, security officers and other staff.

Nurses, physicians, therapists and technologists routinely experience a deep connection to patients and their families. The rest of us should describe our roles in a similar fashion, like my father talked about his role in the military – with pride and with the ability to translate how our job responsibilities enhance our organization's overall mission and reason for existence. We all care for patients and communities.

The iceman and rabbit lady

I love a good story, especially if it's true. Here are two stories I'd like to share with you.

I was chatting with my 92-year-old Aunt Amanda about changes taking place in healthcare. She listened intently at my observations about the challenges and changes taking place. Then she jumped into the conversation with her own story about change and my Uncle Benny, known affectionately to many as the "Iceman." My uncle didn't derive his nickname from being prehistorically set in his ways. And he also wasn't known for having ice-cold nerves that made him immune from stress or pressure, even though he was calm and relaxed. People gave him the moniker of "Iceman" because that's how he made his living – selling blocks of ice.

Uncle Benny built up a loyal customer base and his business flourished because he worked hard to develop relationships with all of his clients.

Uncle Benny delivered ice door-to-door to people's homes. His business predated the electric domestic refrigerator, back when people instead relied upon an icebox in their homes. He charged 5 to 25 cents for his different-sized ice products. He began his daily route in the early morning hours. Uncle Benny built up a loyal customer base and his business flourished because he worked hard to develop relationships with all of his clients.

A colleague relayed the second story to me, describing a meeting he had with an employee who was retiring after 50 years of service in a hospital laboratory. My colleague was chatting with her about the changes she had experienced over her long career. She remembered back to her earliest years with the hospital and described one of her primary job responsibilities – transporting rabbits from an attached building to the lab.

The rabbits were used as standard diagnostic testing tools to help determine if women were pregnant. Here's how the test worked, and pardon my nonclinical explanation. Lab staff would collect a woman's urine sample, inject it into the female rabbit, and then, several days later, study the animal for the presence of a specific hormone. If the hormone was present in the rabbit, then "modern" medicine during that era could scientifically conclude that the patient was pregnant.

This exam was always fatal to the rabbit, despite popular belief that it only died if the woman was indeed pregnant. This testing method gave birth to the phrase "the rabbit died," a colloquial way to announce that a woman was with child. Rabbits were also substituted with white mice and frogs for the test. The lab employee confessed that she always felt bad for the rabbits and mice, less so for the frogs.

That method of testing for pregnancy seems so ancient, just like my Uncle Benny's daily deliveries of ice to people's homes.

I'm confident that someday we'll all be sharing timeworn stories with grandchildren or a group of new team members – odd stories about how we do things today – that will seem ancient to future generations. The jobs of Uncle Benny and the lab supervisor also remind me that our world constantly changes and that we all need to embrace innovation and explore new ways to improve healthcare for generations to come.

Aunt Amanda passed away last August. I will always remember her story about change and Uncle Benny. And I will never forget one of her comments to me. "You have to have a new plan and lots of ideas, because waking up one morning to find out people don't need your blocks of ice is scary."

I'm optimistic we will be innovators at Novant Health. Ideas exist in every department. Be sure to share yours at www.IdeasChangeLives.org, which is our website for sharing and exploring ways to innovate and improve patient care.

My decision now to help my children later

It's incredibly painful to think about the situation in which my children will someday need to make decisions about their mom's and dad's healthcare. It's a somber topic.

My pledge this week is to embrace National Healthcare Decisions Day on Tuesday, April 16. My wife and I took this opportunity to update our advance directives, which had become outdated as our children grew older. I encourage each of you to take the time to think about creating an advance directive or to make sure that yours are up-to-date and reflect your current wishes. Nationally, only 3 in 10 adults have taken the time to create an advance directive.

There are two main types of advance directives:

1. Healthcare power of attorney, where you choose the person you want to make healthcare decisions for you when you cannot speak for yourself;

2. A living will that expresses your wishes about end-of-life care.

Today I want to strongly encourage every Novant Health team member to execute a healthcare power of attorney, no matter what your age or personal circumstance. Here's why.

Creating a healthcare power of attorney means that you've identified someone – whom you trust wholeheartedly – to make healthcare decisions for you if you cannot speak for yourself. Many individuals think about this step as only important for seniors or the terminally ill. However, consider these situations. Who would make decisions while you're sedated during surgery? After a traffic accident if you're unconscious? Or during sudden illness that prevents you from making decisions on your own? By creating a healthcare power of attorney, you can thoughtfully decide now which person you trust to make important healthcare decisions on your behalf.

Every day in one of our facilities, Novant Health staff cares for patients whose families are struggling with decisions about a loved one's care. Our physicians, nurses and staff try to counsel families during these emotional situations, which sometimes exist with a lack of understanding or consensus of the patient's true healthcare wishes. Without the patient having created a healthcare power of attorney, decisions about the individual's care can create long-lasting family turmoil or even necessitate the involvement of the court system.

Last year, my Uncle Gus underwent brain surgery. Many of us thought he'd be returning home and I had already begun construction of a lift and ramp for his home. But his health suddenly deteriorated, resulting in a coma. His more immediate family struggled tremendously with decisions about his care. I'm sure that those tough decisions could have been made a little easier with more advance communication.

I've learned over the years that we must prepare our loved ones for inevitable decisions that are difficult and complex. Please consider that preparation now. Take time to learn more about executing a healthcare power of attorney. Also remember that, despite the document's title, you don't need an attorney to prepare this form.

While I'm not qualified to counsel people about the details of advance directives, Novant Health has staff members who can assist. A good way to start is by visiting I-Connect to find instructions and forms online. And in the months ahead, you will be hearing more about Novant Health efforts to elevate the importance of everyone having an advance directive.

His name was Buster

I'm sure many of you can relate to how I feel about my dog Buster. He was part of our family for 15 years and it's hard to remember life before him. I have almost as many special memories of him as I do of my children. Just because he was a golden retriever doesn't mean we didn't love him and see him as a significant member of the family.

Sadly, Buster passed away a few weeks ago and the loss hit each of us hard. As the patriarch of the family, it was my job to help Buster at the end because it was too painful for everyone else. We had watched him decline for some time but couldn't accept that he was dying. One cold night he went outside and curled up under a chair. I encouraged him to come inside but he didn't have the strength.

I knew it was his time to go, but you know me – I never give up without a fight. I decided to help Buster fight a little longer. I built a fire next to him to keep him warm, hand-fed him peanut butter and gave him water hoping I could reverse the dying

Regardless of the life lived, it's incredibly painful and challenging to let go. We're not ready. We want more time and more experiences with those we love.

process. My wife and I carried him inside and we laid beside him. Buster did perk up after a while. Briefly he was like his younger self, and I was relieved until Buster placed his paw on my arm. He looked at me and I knew it was his time. I knew he needed me to let go. Buster passed away peacefully at the vet's office with my wife holding him.

As heartbreaking as it was to say goodbye to Buster, that grief doesn't even come close to the sorrow I felt when my dad died. Death is so hard. We lose loved ones even if they have fought valiantly to stay with us. Some are taken before their time and others have lived long and full lives. Regardless of the life lived, it's incredibly painful and challenging to let go. We're not ready. We want more time and more experiences with those we love.

Unfortunately, sometimes we won't even talk about death because we hope we can put it off or avoid it until we're ready. Most people don't like to think about, much less talk about, what could happen, especially when they are young with many things still to accomplish. Unfortunately, this often results in not knowing a person's wishes when an accident or tragedy happens. Loved ones aren't sure how to make decisions when the patient is unconscious, even if recovery isn't anticipated. This uncertainty sometimes rips families apart when they need one another the most.

That's why I urge everyone to make an advance directive, which is a formal document outlining your healthcare wishes in situations where you are unable to speak for yourself. This week, which is National Healthcare Decisions week, we are launching Choices and Champions – a program designed to help people start the conversation with their loved ones. It includes materials to help you make your choices and choose your champions – the people you trust to be involved in your care. We'll also help you create your advance directives so your wishes can be legally honored.

As part of our effort to create awareness of end-of-life issues, we also will participate in a global campaign launched by artist Candy Chang a few years ago. If you are not familiar with Candy Chang, you might want to watch her TED talk to learn more. Her story is very powerful. She placed graffiti-style boards titled "Before I die" in communities and encouraged people to talk about what they want to do before they die – a one-line "bucket list." This simple exercise helps folks think about and have conversations with others about things that matter – how we want to make the most of the time we have left.

Whom do you trust to make healthcare decisions for you? What do you think makes life worth living? What do you want to do before you die?

Because we believe these issues are so important, we are sharing Choices and Champions with our team members first before we publicly share this with our patients. I encourage you to visit the Choices and Champions website. Take the time to make your choices and choose your champion today. Leaving this world peacefully and gracefully is just one lesson I learned from Buster. Helping my family prepare so they know when to let go is another.

Getting back into the swing of things

The last few weeks have been nice for me since I had surgery 19 weeks ago. My new right ankle and I were cleared to exercise so I'm back on the elliptical working out. I'm up to 35 minutes of exercise a day.

My ankle fusion didn't require significant rehabilitation because I'm not supposed to bend the ankle. That means I've been inactive for a while now, and it's going to take time to build up my endurance to work out for a full hour. To improve my strength and balance, squats and leg presses have also become part of my exercise routine.

I'm also walking longer distances, which means I'm finally back to rounding. Last week I was at Novant Health Rowan Medical Center and Novant Health Forsyth Medical Center, and the week before that I visited the team at Novant Health Brunswick Medical Center. It feels good to be out and about again.

Since my surgery, I've learned what it's like to rely on others while I recuperated. A big milestone for me was when I got the green light to drive. Since November, my wife, Christi, has driven me everywhere. She's taken me to early meetings in Winston-Salem, Charlotte and Salisbury. Anywhere I needed to go, she chauffeured me. And truth be told, she's probably the one person more excited than I was to see me driving again! I'm still thanking her, because at times I wasn't the best passenger.

And my first few times I was behind the wheel, I realized driving without bending my ankle was going to require some careful maneuvering. Not able to push the top of my foot forward to accelerate, I had to reposition the seat and pedals so I could push the accelerator with my entire foot. It's amazing what you take for granted when you're in good health.

My goal now is to be ready to tee up for Novant Health Hemby Children's Hospital Golf Classic coming up later this month. I'm looking forward to enjoying the day at the golf tournament with our team members and the people who support us. And I'm hoping my return to the tennis court isn't far behind.

I'm finally mobile and independent again. I now have a deeper appreciation for the ability to walk. A year ago, walking was a chore for me. Now it's a pleasure, something I no longer take for granted.

Likewise, I also appreciate the team members at Novant Health Charlotte Orthopedic Hospital and Novant Health

Cotswold Medical Clinic who have helped me get back on track. From the physicians to nurses to everyone else who helped me during my recovery, thank you. I wouldn't feel this good without you.

Louis left a legacy of love

Big-hearted, fun-loving and a family man all the way through: That describes my Uncle Louis. A Louisiana native committed to his community – whether he was coaching, working in his insurance business, or serving the town and on the school board – Uncle Louis had a way of drawing people to himself. He wasn't just the life of the party; he *was* the party. And he was deeply instrumental in my life.

We lost Uncle Louis in October. Many of you come to this holiday week missing a beloved person in your own circle of family or friends, so you know what that's like. That's why I want to remind all of us, whether in holiday celebrations or in our facilities caring for patients, to be fully present with those around us.

The thing is, we never know how much time we'll have with someone we care about. And small moments are ones to celebrate: taking a walk in the crisp winter air or sitting around the table telling funny stories. We're all very busy, and it's easy to be lured into the myth of multitasking. It's easy to look at our phones more than we look into the faces of those around us.

Let's embrace the time we spend with family and friends, distraction-free. When we give others our full presence, we are showing them that they matter. That's something I see in all of our facilities, where many of you will be caring for patients and their

We're all very busy, and it's easy to be lured into the myth of multitasking. It's easy to look at our phones more than we look into the faces of those around us.

families throughout the holidays, sacrificing your time to serve others. I've seen how so many of you take time to make those patients feel important, to give deeply of yourself.

That's what my uncle did. When you were with him, he made you feel important. He was interested in the lives of his children, his grandchildren – and nephews like me. He invested in others and left a legacy of love – a legacy that each of us can leave, too, in both our personal lives and the lives of our patients.

This holiday season, I'm missing my uncle, but I'm excited about the opportunity to carry on what he modeled throughout his life. And I'm so thankful for all of you, and for all that you do to build that same kind of legacy at Novant Health. Happy holidays! Merry Christmas! Happy Hanukkah! Happy Kwanzaa!

Make your January resolution to open a door

There he was, crossing the stage to shake hands with the dean of the college congratulating him on successfully graduating. As I watched my son graduate from college this month, I felt a thrill many of you have, seeing a young person officially turn the page to the next chapter in his or her life.

I'm proud of all three of my children, but there's nothing like a graduation to make you reflect and be filled with gratitude not just for all that's been achieved, but for all that is yet to come. There's something almost electrifying about the opportunity to start something new. A commencement ceremony reminds us to reflect on what it took to get where we are and to focus on the future – to honor our past while charting a bold new course for tomorrow.

And while college graduation is a big milestone, the wonderful thing is that we don't need a milestone to change direction. January represents a powerful moment to begin anew.

This isn't about making a resolution; it's about moving through an open door. A door that leads to new opportunities to make life better for our patients, teammates and our communities, to serve them with passion and creativity. A door that leads to the chance to renew connections to family and friends. And even a door leading to a better version of ourselves – one achieved through taking small, brave steps of improvement.

Celebrating a graduation also reminded me that we need to make time to celebrate all new beginnings. Starting on a new path is exciting, but it also can be hard. That's why it's important to honor the effort in ourselves and others. We all need encouragement as we make change. I've noticed that the team here at Novant Health is particularly good at this. You regularly share stories about how you cheer one another on as you challenge yourselves to improve personally and professionally.

We learn from the past, cherish its good memories and weave it into the story of who we are. But life is about growing and moving forward. It's about walking through the open door of a new year, into the unknown, with determination and hope. Here's to 2017 – and the opportunities that await each of us!

Hope for a cure for type 1 diabetes

I was honored this past weekend to participate in the 2017 JDRF Hope Gala in Winston-Salem, an event dedicated to raising money for type 1 diabetes research. It was an exciting event because it brought together so many people focused on the crucial cause of finding a cure for this condition.

Type 1 diabetes, as most of you know, is an autoimmune disease that can strike people of any age, and is unrelated to diet or lifestyle. JDRF is the leading global organization funding research into the condition and it's a group I'm passionate about. So many people have better lives today because of the work JDRF does. I'm one of them.

As I've shared in this space before, I was diagnosed at 18 months with type 1 diabetes. My mother had to give me life-sustaining insulin shots until I was old enough to do it. My mom

Some 1.25 million Americans live with
type 1 diabetes and with the constant vigilance
it requires.

and dad showed me how to manage my disease. And, as I shared in my speech to the JDRF last weekend, my parents taught me to see life as a set of possibilities to be embraced, rather than a series of worries to be feared.

That's a stance the JDRF supports. JDRF educates people about living a full life with the condition and provides much-needed support for patients and their families. Just like we are at Novant Health, it's working to make people healthier.

Some 1.25 million Americans live with type 1 diabetes and with the constant vigilance it requires. The JDRF Hope Gala was a reminder that there is indeed hope for people with type 1 diabetes and that it is possible that a cure for this condition will be found.

And my hope is grounded in something fundamental, not only to the valuable work JDRF is doing but also to the work we do every day here at Novant Health. It's this: the belief that a group of passionate, dedicated people who have a bias toward action can accomplish so much together. It's what I believe, it's why I support JDRF, and it's what we're about at Novant Health.

Aunt Amanda taught me a lot, but I'm still learning

She passed away at age 91. Over the years, I learned a lot from Aunt Amanda, as well as other older adults, relatives and neighbors. But my learning seems like it's just beginning.

Our nursing leadership recently shared with me some provocative thoughts about our aging population and challenges we must solve in caring for them.

We are experiencing an unprecedented growth in the number of older adults in the United States. During the next 25 years, the number of Americans 65 and older will double to 72 million. That dramatic surge exists for two main reasons:

1. We're living longer.

2. Infants from the post-WWII baby boom have grown up and are now entering their senior years.

Several discrepancies have developed in parallel to the boom of senior citizens. Experts estimate that only 15 percent of healthcare providers receive any training in geriatrics. More providers are trained in pediatrics, despite the overwhelming number of seniors compared to children. Older patients are also less likely to be tested or screened for diseases and other health problems. There are other fascinating trends; these are just a few.

I was pleased several weeks ago when an email popped up on my Novant Health computer with the subject line of "Ageism Part 1," an online class about care without elderly bias. In addition, several more classes are being planned, designed to debunk stereotypes about the elderly, address "elderspeak" (patronizing or babylike talk to seniors), explore communication predicaments of older adults, delve into wellness for seniors and cover other topics. This series resulted from great collaboration by staff from nursing, diversity, clinical improvement and corporate education.

While these classes are designed for nurses and other healthcare providers, they can benefit every staff member at Novant Health. All of us know one or more people living their elder years. We personally listen to their challenges. Some of us might be involved in helping them stay independent. We might witness others treating them inappropriately. And in many cases, we hopefully enjoy seeing older loved ones living their dream years with gusto and spontaneity, like my Aunt Amanda did.

Please consider participating. These classes are a great jump-start to all the work ahead of us to make healthcare remarkable for our elderly patients, and for everyone.

Seizing the moment to change someone forever

My son recently visited the newly opened Novant Health Clemmons Medical Center. John wasn't attending the festive grand opening – he visited the emergency room after his four-wheeler hit a pothole, injuring his wrist.

You might remember from a past blog post of mine that I, too, recently visited a Novant Health emergency room. I'd like to disclose that it's not my family's intention to try out each and every facility of ours. After all, our health system consists of 500 locations.

My son is doing great. John had outpatient surgery to repair his broken left wrist at Novant Health Charlotte Orthopedic Hospital. He's bummed, though, because the mishap occurred during his first week home from college summer break.

In the scope of all the things that can go wrong during a child's or teenager's life, John's wrist injury could be labeled as "lite." In contrast, we far too often learn about someone else's tragedy that forces us to pause and more deeply appreciate the people we care about.

During his visit to Clemmons Medical Center, the staff gave our family a special gift that was above and beyond the remarkable care he received. It was a gift that caused us to pause and reflect.

What did staff do? They seized the moment to remind John how lucky he is. They asked him not once, not twice, but at least five times if he was wearing a helmet: first a medical center security officer, then a nurse, a physician ... the question kept coming. John admitted that he wasn't wearing one.

At one point during his visit, John said he felt like pinning a sign to himself that read "No, I wasn't wearing a helmet!" to preemptively answer the question from the next wave of staff he would encounter.

I think parents would agree that advice from someone else – a person other than a mom or dad – often has a better chance of sticking and being remembered. The Clemmons staff were the "someone else." John certainly heard the message that day, over and over again from a group of professional staff and clinicians who collectively made their point.

My son certainly realized that questions about helmet usage had nothing to do with the care and treatment for his wrist injury. That's one of the reasons the message was so powerful.

I recognize that not every patient is receptive to advice and lectures of a compassionate nature. I'm sure some of you have experienced those exceptions. But part of our mission and our brand promise is to help people stay healthy, which might include strong encouragement to lose weight, stop smoking, eat more fiber or wear a helmet.

As a father, I'd like to thank the physicians, nurses and the entire team who cared for John at Clemmons Medical Center and Charlotte Orthopedic Hospital. As both a dad and CEO, I'd like to thank all of our Novant Health team members who take the opportunity to deliver the right message, at the right time – in our ERs, nursing units, clinics and outpatient centers. Those moments can change lives forever.

I campaigned for Gus and the power of one vote

Early on in life, I learned about the importance of government, representation and the privilege to vote. My Uncle Gus served as mayor of a small Louisiana town for about 10 years. As a teenager, I helped him campaign by putting signs up around the community and doing whatever I could for my uncle. I enjoyed helping Uncle Gus. In addition, my Uncle Louis served on a local school board in the bayou state where I grew up.

Novant Health is participating in "We Care. We Vote," sponsored by the American Hospital Association, to encourage the millions of our nation's healthcare employees to vote in the upcoming election. Staff members in clinics and hospitals possess a passion for serving patients and a deep commitment to our communities. That devotion can also play a significant role in selecting our government leaders.

Few rights are more fundamentally American than the right to vote; yet many individuals don't take the opportunity to make their voices heard. In the last presidential election, only 58 percent of our country's population voted, according to the U.S. Census Bureau. The reasons are as diverse as our nation, ranging from not knowing how or where to register to vote to dissatisfaction with the political process.

During our nation's relatively young history, many of our community members have defended our freedoms and helped those in other parts of the world either preserve or gain their rights to vote. Since so many people have defended this freedom, often at great personal sacrifice, I feel an obligation to participate in as many elections as I can.

Please take the time to learn about the candidates and issues in this year's election. It's a critical year, and the individuals we elect will make important decisions concerning the future of healthcare and, ultimately, the future of our health system. You have an important role in choosing who gets to make these decisions: our nation's president, a U.S. senator in Virginia, our federal congressmen and congresswomen in all states, North Carolina's governor, state legislators and other elected officials.

The individuals we elect are true servants. And they can dramatically affect our environment of patient care and clinical practice. Their decisions determine our payments from Medicare and Medicaid, which in turn affect the resources we have to serve our patients and communities. Their decisions influence our ability to expand and build facilities, such as our emergency departments, diagnostic imaging centers and hospitals. Their decisions can either limit or expand a clinician's scope of practice. And the list goes on.

Form your own opinions and then cast your vote on Nov. 6. You hold the power, and the privilege, of voting to make a difference. Don't squander the opportunity.

Bringing everyone to the table

There's something wonderful about a big family dinner. It's much more than the meal. It's the presence of everyone around the table, the wide-ranging conversation, the different perspectives, the unique contributions of each person. Sure, sometimes there's tension, but what I think about most are all of the voices, the stories – and how, at the end of the meal, you feel filled in a way that has nothing to do with the food.

That's the image I carry in my mind when I think about our team at Novant Health. We hold up diversity and inclusion as a core value, not only because it's the right thing to do, but because we can only be the organization we want to be – to fulfill our calling – by including the strengths and talents of each person. The communities we serve are diverse, and we want to be welcoming to all people.

On a recent listening tour throughout the system, Tanya Blackmon, executive vice president and chief diversity and inclusion officer, heard a lot of hopeful stories from team members about how our efforts to have a diverse workforce and create an inclusive environment are working. We're also implementing a strategic plan to truly embed diversity and inclusion throughout the organization.

Allow me to highlight some aspects of the strategic plan: We've added three women to the Novant Health executive team

... we can only be the organization we want to be – to fulfill our calling – by including the strengths and talents of each person.

to better reflect our workforce and are creating a program to assist female team members in career development. We're updating materials used in our diversity and inclusion classes, and that new material will be used in the fourth quarter. The executive team is participating in educational sessions to deepen our understanding of the factors that impact team members and our patients. Our business resource groups are spearheading a wide range of exciting projects, from creating a Spanish-language microsite (a component of the Novant Health website) for our Latino patients to hosting an event this month in Winston-Salem with Damon Tweedy, MD, author of *Black Man in a White Coat: A Doctor's Reflections on Race and Medicine*.

Developing programs is a component of embedding diversity and inclusion, and programs provide great opportunities to enrich our understanding. But it all begins with us as individuals, getting to know our colleagues and their backgrounds, interests, personalities and worldviews. As Tanya puts it, "Understanding people is our business. In healthcare, if we don't understand our patient population and our team members, then we don't have a business. We have to understand the needs of all people better than anybody else."

I'm proud of the work we're doing to make Novant Health richly diverse and warmly inclusive – a place where we're bringing everyone to the table.

Section 8

Waking up love and supporting values on holidays

A Thanksgiving toast for Ty

This Thanksgiving, a Winston-Salem family will celebrate the holiday because Ty, one of our security officers, ignored his job. And lots of people, including me, are glad he did.

Ty serves as a security officer at Novant Health Forsyth Medical Center. During one of his shifts this past summer, he noticed smoke coming from a housing complex across the street. Ty investigated and found flames rising up from trees and shrubs alongside the wooden apartment building. The fire was beginning to reach the outside walls, so he ran upstairs to alert residents.

Along the way, Ty spotted a young girl standing in an apartment doorway, where she lived with her elderly grandparents. Someone was already calling 911, so Ty and the family began to think of ways to put out the fire. Ty discovered that the outside faucet didn't work, so searching for a hose wouldn't help. He also noticed that the family's apartment kitchen had several large plastic containers. He began filling them up using the kitchen sink and raced outside to douse the largest flames. The girl, maybe 11 or 12 years old, refilled the emptied containers while Ty sprinted back and forth to fight the fire.

As others scrambled to move their cars away from the building, Ty and his young accomplice continued to extinguish the fire by filling and refilling containers. When the fire department arrived, most of the flames were out and the firefighters took over the remaining challenge.

Thanks to Ty's quick and selfless actions, a lot of damage was averted and families were spared the potential tragedy that often accompanies fire disasters. After several hugs and handshakes, Ty returned to work at his Novant Health post.

What are you thankful for this year? At the Thanksgiving table this year, I will cherish family, friends and health, as well as the Novant Health team members who work on this holiday to care for our patients. And I know with certainty that people are grateful for Ty and that they're toasting him during their holiday meal and celebration.

Honoring the strong women in our lives

All of us have someone in our lives to celebrate on Mother's Day, a mom or other woman who has made a difference in our lives. I always honor my mom along with my wife, Christi, and my mother-in-law. These three women have dedicated their lives to making a lasting impression on the world through working outside the home, working inside the home and raising children.

Today, I'd like to pay a short tribute to the person who has influenced my life more than any other: my mom. She is a genuine people person who cares about others as much as she cares about her family.

Her approach to motherhood was to aim to raise three boys who were kind and respectful. She taught us manners and how to say "I'm sorry." In fact, my brothers and I learned early that forgiving was the only way to live life. Holding a grudge was not an option. Mom also taught us compassion and showed us how to make ourselves available for those in need, whether they are friends, family members or strangers.

Somehow, Mom was always there when I needed her. She was there to clean and bandage scraped knees after a bike wreck. She provided the pep talk following a rough day on the baseball field. And she was my caretaker and confidante who helped me recuperate from a serious car accident that shattered my ankle in college. And between the hugs and encouragement, she provided firm discipline without being overbearing.

Perhaps one of the best life lessons that she taught me was to take risks. It was a given that sometimes you will fail, and she reassured me that was OK. Don't be afraid to do so. Succeeding is about not being afraid to live life. And it's also about being open to change and balancing the risk. If you fail, then stay positive.

Of course, being positive is central to who I am. That's a trait I inherited from Mom. She taught me to graciously handle the bad experiences along with the good ones. In fact, she would argue that the determination to focus on the positive is what separates those who succeed from those who fail. At the end of day, count your blessings, she said, because focusing on the good in life is the best way to live.

I am grateful for this woman because I am a better person because of her. Thank you, Mom, for all that you do for me.

I also appreciate the strong, creative women at Novant Health. More than 80 percent of our team members are women, and many of them were working on Mother's Day while their colleagues were spending part of their day with loved ones. I thank you all – mothers, sisters, daughters, grandmothers, granddaughters, partners and friends – who make Novant Health the great place that it is.

So who are some of the strong women who have helped shape your life? I would love to hear your stories!

We owe them remembrance and service

When someone sacrifices his or her own interests to serve us, it makes a lasting impression. And when someone gives up a life to serve others, that's something we should never forget.

My dad, Lucien Armato, didn't talk much about his four years of service in the Army. He was a man dedicated to his family and to making the most of the present moment. He didn't see combat but was honored to serve, both in those military years and over the course of his entire life. Something that amazes me about my dad: Each morning he woke up thinking about which people he could serve that day.

My dad passed away in 1996, and so many people came to celebrate the impact he made that we actually had to hold two services because there was standing room only. He's the person I often find myself thinking about on Memorial Day, our holiday to honor those who died in service for their country. While my father was able to return to his family after his service, so many others didn't – and still don't.

A tension exists around this special holiday. There's the sacred duty to honor those who make the ultimate sacrifice for America. And there's the other pull – to enjoy the moment and live our lives as they would have surely lived theirs, if they'd had the chance.

That's why I don't think there's anything wrong with the way most of us enjoy Memorial Day when we are not at work serving patients – by gathering with those we love to share a meal. To break bread with people we care about, to enjoy the beautiful outdoors, to laugh and make memories – those simple things are part of the fabric of this good life.

There's really no contradiction in sweet moments with family and friends taking place on a day that honors the fallen. Joy always exists alongside pain. What I think the day calls us to do is simple: to remember. We remember those we cherished who fought and died. We remember the service of people we never knew personally, and we honor them.

We may not be called into military service, but we're all called to serve. We serve our patients and one another. We serve our families and communities. We sacrifice to make someone else's life a little better. We can start our mornings, like my father did, asking ourselves whom we might serve that day. On Memorial Day we celebrate, serve – and remember. It's what we owe those who gave all.

We remember those we cherished who fought and died. We remember the service of people we never knew personally, and we honor them.

Staffers infuse holiday spirit into their work

Many people celebrate holidays, including the New Year, at this time of year, with some of our team members already taking time off for celebrations at home or far away. I hope all of you will be surrounded by love and warmth at these special occasions and enjoy them to the fullest. I'm looking forward to getting together with family and friends for a lot of conversation, laughter and good food.

While holiday traditions bring joy to most people, health challenges dampen the season for others. And knowing their needs can't wait, we're ready to help. We understand that holidays are included when delivering the most remarkable care experience, in every dimension, every time.

We also recognize that our patients would rather be home for the holidays, so it's the perfect time to add a few extra touches in how we care for them. Robin, a clinical support coordinator at Novant Health Forsyth Medical Center, provides a great example. She worked on the most recent Thanksgiving Day, as she has for the past seven years, because it's why she entered the medical field – to put the needs of others ahead of her own. Robin does small things for her patients that make a big difference. When a patient wanted to look her best for family members coming to visit, Robin helped fix her hair and apply makeup. She also noticed patients who didn't have any visitors and spent time with them, chatting about their interests and seeing if there was anything she could do to brighten their day.

Working together as a family and treating patients like family are common themes when our team members talk about their on-the-job holiday experiences. Mary, an emergency department tech at Novant Health UVA Health System Prince William Medical Center, started Thanksgiving Day enjoying a potluck breakfast at work with her "family away from home." During the day, Mary paid extra attention to the comfort of patients' family members who had their holiday interrupted by an unwanted trip to the emergency room. She helped one patient stop worrying about how the family's holiday meal would be prepared by reassuring the patient's husband that he could leave to start cooking as his wife's treatment would be completed in a couple of hours and she could return home then.

I applaud such devotion and appreciate everyone on our team who works on the holidays. You're there for our patients when needed and you're using your creativity to add something a little special to the day. I thank all of you for your dedication to our brand promise throughout the year. I've seen a lot of examples of caring and giving behavior that is not an occasional event at Novant Health. It happens all the time. Thank you for bringing that commitment to your role every day. It's a wonderful and amazing gift that you've chosen to share.

Thanking those who work the holidays

Now is a busy and joyous time for many as we officially enter the final two weeks of the year. Odds are good you've already enjoyed a holiday get-together or two. And once the kids are home from school, from the young ones in kindergarten all the way up to college students, winter break is in full swing.

December is always a special time at the Armato house. Decorations set the spirited mood. Lots of food is fixed for the festivities. Family members arrive from out of state, and plenty of laughter and love fills the house for several days.

And starting this week, some team members will take their well-deserved paid time off. Many of us celebrate different holidays this month: Hanukkah, Christmas, Kwanzaa, the New Year. But we all know that healthcare never shuts down, not even during important celebrations.

Thank you for providing remarkable patient care on these days – and in doing so, allowing others to enjoy the company of those closest to them.

The doors to our medical centers remain open to all who need care, so thank you to our care teams in the emergency rooms and the inpatient units as well as our support teams in food services, patient safety, environmental services and other areas that serve so well. These colleagues are working so others can have their special day – or several days – off.

I appreciate the dedication and devotion of all team members, but those who work through the holidays deserve extra recognition. Thank you for providing remarkable patient care on these days – and in doing so, allowing others to enjoy the company of those closest to them.

Thank you!

The "can do" that makes our nation remarkable

I t was quite a way to celebrate a 21st birthday.

Rachel Smith marked that milestone while stationed near the Iraqi border during Operation Desert Storm. There, she alternated days treating the sick and wounded at the 28th Combat Support Hospital with nights on perimeter guard duty, listening to Scud missiles explode.

Rachel was a licensed practical nurse at the time, serving in the U.S. Army. Her experience in the Gulf War taught her to conquer chaos with calm, to face adversity with determined discipline. She cared for American soldiers and Iraqi prisoners of war alike, recognizing all as people in need of her help. Rachel said those lessons translate very well to her current role as a nurse manager of behavioral health at Novant Health UVA Health System.

"The connection is 'can do,'" said Rachel. "'Can do' was the motto of our unit. It's not about how I'm going to achieve a goal – I just think about the objective. And camaraderie is huge – just getting along in support of the mission and putting our differences aside to get our job done."

This week, we make time to honor our veterans for the sacrifices they have made and continue to make in service to our country. Veterans contribute so much to our organization and to the compassionate care our patients receive. And they often say that their time in the military shapes their perspective on our mission.

That's the case with Mark Higdon, DO, director of the Novant Health Family Medicine Residency Program. Dr. Higdon served in the Army for 25 years, retiring as a colonel. First, he flew as a pilot during Desert Storm. Then he returned to Iraq in 2005 as a doctor, supporting the 4th Sustainment Brigade.

"There were a lot of people getting hurt, a lot of death and destruction, but the medicine was the same," Dr. Higdon said. "The vast majority of the medicine was primary care, interspersed with tremendous trauma."

The military, says Dr. Higdon, is a team – many professional individuals are required to be successful. "It's very much like the team we have here at Novant Health," he said. "I was very proud of my service when I was in uniform, but I have to confess I am equally proud of what I do now."

I am so grateful for all of the veterans who work in each of our facilities, sharing the skills they sharpened while in service to our nation and enriching all of our teams with their experiences. You have given so much. This week, and every week, please know that you have our thanks and gratitude!

Carve out some time for gratitude

Thanksgiving is a time of traditions, some longstanding – extended families and friends gathering together, Grandma's pumpkin pie recipe, the pull of a nap after a big meal – and some newer, formed as our families and lives change and grow.

Many people have a tradition of going around the table and mentioning something for which they are grateful. It's a nice way of reviewing the past year and acknowledging all the good in our lives, everything from health to jobs to great football weather.

Research supports what we know intuitively – that regularly expressing gratitude lifts our spirits and gives us a more optimistic outlook on life. And what I'd like to suggest is that this week, we take that idea and make it even more specific. Let's think about a person or people in our lives for whom we are grateful – and let those folks know.

Maybe you had a teacher who inspired you to stretch beyond what you thought were your limitations. Perhaps a family member helped you through a hard time. Maybe you have a team member here at Novant Health who has encouraged you, listened to you, taught you something new. I know from my visits to our facilities that there are stories everywhere of the way you have lifted up one another, sparking creativity, reaching out to extend a helping hand, and offering kindness when it was especially needed.

Sometimes we feel grateful for someone, but that thanks goes unsaid. We get busy, or maybe we feel a little awkward. Any number of things can stop us from writing a note or simply turning to someone and saying, "Thank you for all you're doing."

But here's the thing: Life is short. And life can be hard. We need all the encouragement we can get from one another. We have so many people in our lives who are quietly making a difference, and we should let them know that.

I encourage each of us to take a moment to turn to a colleague here at Novant Health and offer a word of thanks. Let's all express our thanks to those who have offered us gifts of wisdom, friendship, guidance and even laughter.

I'll start with mine: Thank you to all of you in our organization for your dedication and teamwork in helping our patients lead healthier lives. Happy Thanksgiving!

Jewelry? Computer? Candy? Or attention?

We're into the holiday season now, often a time of joy and reflection. But it also can be a difficult season for those who are struggling with a health issue or who have lost a family member. That's why, no matter what your December tradition, it's an important time to give one of the best gifts of all: your attention.

It's a gift that requires no standing in line, costs nothing and needs no wrapping. The only thing this gift requires is our time. Maybe you work with someone who has lost a family member and is facing the first holiday season without that loved one. Perhaps there's a patient struggling with difficult health news. People who are hurting often feel they are alone. Notice their needs – say a kind word, offer help above and beyond your job description, drop a card in the mail that lets that person know you care.

There's an old saying in the world of sales that says the most important word a salesperson can say to a prospective customer is the customer's name. I think that's because at heart, we want to be noticed; we want to be known. We want to be assured that someone is paying attention to the things going on in our lives.

This month, let's make a point to recognize the needs of the

That's why, no matter what your December tradition, it's an important time to give one of the best gifts of all: your attention.

people around us and show our compassion in a tangible way. The new parent who is dealing with sleeplessness, the person grieving the loss of a spouse, the child spending the holidays in the hospital – they and others in need represent opportunities for giving a gift that will make an impact far beyond the holiday season. I think we all know this. Most of us can probably recall a note, a hand on a shoulder, a word of empathy at just the right time – things that might have happened long ago but whose memory we still cherish.

One of the things that brings me the most pride about Novant Health is that it's an organization with a heart. You, our Novant Health team members, show all the time that you care deeply about our patients and one another. It is part of what makes our organization different. This season, let's use that strength to give the gift of attention to the people around us – a gift we can all celebrate!

From the battlefield to life with gratitude

As we celebrate Thanksgiving this week, I'm reminded again of the fact that when we practice gratitude, it can shape the way we live – and change countless lives for the better.

That's certainly been the case for Doc, now 91, who nearly died on a World War II battlefield. He's made a habit of grateful giving ever since – a habit that will benefit patients at Novant Health Kernersville Medical Center, whose team shared Doc's story with me.

Doc remembers every detail of that day on the French battlefield. When he hit the ground, Doc knew he was seriously wounded. A second shot aimed at his heart struck instead a small Bible he always kept in his breast pocket, and the shrapnel lodged in the final pages. All during the dark night Doc, part of the U.S. 79th Infantry Division, listened to the cries of the wounded men around him and prayed for rescue.

Against long odds, Doc survived. He came home to propose to his high school sweetheart, Doris, and lived to raise a family and build a thriving transportation business. Doc says that after a lifetime of blessings, it's become second nature to give to others anytime he can – especially within the community that nurtured him and his business for so many years. It's this impulse that led Doc to give a gift to the Novant Health Kernersville Medical Center Foundation general fund. Kernersville Medical Center dedicated its chapel to his wife, Doris, who passed away in 1990.

"I'd visited Novant Health Kernersville Medical Center before I gave my gift and I'd never been at a hospital where the staff was as nice as they were to me," Doc says. "I saw the need for helping the hospital here in Kernersville and I was just happy I could help in a small way."

As many of us gather with family and friends to celebrate Thanksgiving, let's make a point to keep the gratitude going. Maybe you haven't faced death the way Doc did, but we all have something large or small for which we can be grateful. Gratitude shifts our attention away from what we lack to all that we have. It makes us happier. It reminds us that life is a gift.

Among the many things for which I'm grateful: the entire team at Novant Health. You all put so much of yourselves into your jobs every day, and it shows. No matter what your job here is, you are making people's lives better as a result. Thank you for that.

Happy Thanksgiving!

The holiday joy of going full throttle

December always ends up being a memorable time of year for me. It's been a great month. It started out with my mom and mother-in-law traveling to North Carolina a couple of weeks before Christmas. One Sunday, I decided to take both of them to some land I own near Winston-Salem. We took a leisurely walk through the woods and reminisced about my youth and their grandkids.

While we were there, I thought it would be a great idea to take my mom riding on an all-terrain vehicle. She said she had no desire to take such an adventure. She added that she was doing just fine "two-footing" it down the trail. But with some coaxing, I managed to take her for a ride in an ATV with two seats. With a lot more coaxing, I managed to get her into the driver's seat. I showed her how to work the throttle and how to brake. She was busy arguing with me that people her age shouldn't be riding ATVs. I kept telling her that was ridiculous; just give it a chance.

Before I knew it, she was going full throttle on a level stretch of the trail, and I couldn't help but notice that the smile on her face was one of pure joy. It was a real thrill to see Mom experiencing something new and exciting in her 70s.

As the holiday grew nearer, more family arrived. Mid-December brought my college-age daughter and son home for winter break, reuniting them with their younger brother. Then as Christmas Eve rolled around, we had more than 20 family members under one roof. We filled every bed and couch in the house as well as a lot of floor space. Perhaps the best gift this year was we had four generations under one roof. It doesn't get much better than that.

Once the house emptied and family members left for home, I made my way back to Forsyth County to take a walk in the woods by myself. There really is nothing quite like it when you're alone with nature. When I'm in North Carolina, it's in the timbered rolling hills. When I'm in Louisiana, it's on the water. I love to get far enough away that you can hear only the sounds of nature. No traffic. No distant horns of freight trains. This quiet time allows me to really relax and focus on the future.

My month has been about appreciating my family, focusing on what's important and looking forward toward what's to come. I've pretty much gone from going full throttle to idling, and I'm now ready to shift into overdrive for the New Year – the perfect time to renew our commitment to our promise and the remarkable patient experience for our Novant Health family.

Not just a day for grilling outside

Today, I hope you will join me in remembering all those who have died in military service for our nation.

Everyone honors Memorial Day a little differently. For many, it's a holiday that includes picnics or grilling out in a backyard or park. People attend parades or other special events. For some families, the holiday always includes a visit to a cemetery to mark gravestones with flowers or an American flag.

Several of our facilities hold their own Memorial Day ceremonies to honor all branches of the military: men and women still serving, veterans and those in our memories. Many people also work on this Monday holiday, like staff of our health system and medical centers.

On this Memorial Day, join me in thanking all those who serve in our military. If you'd like an additional way to remember someone today, please feel free to share a name or personal comment on this blog. And look up to the flags on our main campuses this morning – they'll be flying at half-mast from sunrise to noon.

The wedding ring and a future Mother's Day

In honor of Mother's Day this coming Sunday, I'd like to share two patient stories with you. One reminds me that the little things in life matter a lot, and the other story puts the entirety of life in proper perspective.

Jackie works in the emergency department at Novant Health Rowan Medical Center and she shared the story of her mother-in-law's care. Her mother-in-law became critically ill and Jackie brought her to Rowan Medical Center, where she was admitted to the intensive care unit. Jackie described the warmth and compassion from staff anytime a family member called or visited. Her family especially appreciated the explanations of what to expect in care and treatment.

*Then, with extraordinary effort and some "magic"
by the nurses, they removed the patient's rings in
one piece and safely stored them for the family.*

Jackie also explained that her mother-in-law experienced severe swelling in her hands, which required the decision to cut off her wedding rings before permanent damaged occurred to her finger. Jackie described how heartbroken everyone was – the rings meant a lot to her mother-in-law who wore them as a continuous reminder of her husband who'd passed away. Jackie could not remember a single time when her mother-in-law had removed her rings. Then, with extraordinary effort and some "magic" by the nurses, they removed the patient's rings in one piece and safely stored them for the family.

Her mother-in-law could not speak that day because of her medical condition, but Jackie knows that she would have emotionally thanked the hospital staff for saving something little that meant a lot.

The other story begins with a young family's nightmare. Two weeks after giving birth, a mother experienced chest pains at home and was rushed by ambulance to Novant Health Matthews Medical Center. She had no medical history of heart disease.

Minutes after arriving to the emergency department, she became unresponsive, with no pulse. Staff performed multiple rounds of defibrillation as the patient's condition continued to deteriorate. She was shocked nine times in the emergency room and additional times in the cardiac catheterization lab. A quick decision was then made to transfer her; she was defibrillated again several times by the Novant Health Critical Care Transport team as they rushed her to Novant Health Presbyterian Medical Center. Upon arrival, she underwent emergency open heart surgery.

Today, the mother has fully recovered. She expressed to staff how grateful she is and how she looks forward to future birthdays, anniversaries, graduations and weddings. And she especially values this Mother's Day with her newborn, 2-year-old daughter, husband and family.

To all of the mothers reading this post, enjoy your special celebration this Sunday. We're all thankful for your devotion to nurturing others. And a special thank you goes out to all the mothers who are working that day.

Waking up love

Many holidays are smothered in one common emotion: love.

The holidays associated with December certainly reflect this emotion. I can also see the same passion in other holidays, such as the love for nation on the Fourth of July and love for mothers and fathers on their special days.

The word also defines the accomplishment of several staff members who recently uplifted the holiday season for a patient and her loved one. I was in awe after hearing this story.

A Novant Health Forsyth Medical Center nurse was caring for a terminally ill patient who had been unconscious for several days. The chances of the patient awakening again were very poor. In prior months, the patient and her partner struggled with the fairly recent cancer diagnosis, like most couples would. Confiding in the nurse, the partner shared one wish for the holidays and the final few days – to hear the patient say "I love you" one more time.

The partner eventually went home to get some rest. When the nurse returned the next evening to work, she expected to learn that the patient had passed away. But surprisingly, as the nurse walked into the room, her terminally ill patient was awake and speaking. The nurse calmed the anxious patient and asked if she'd like to see her partner. The patient's face lit up as she heard her partner's name. Then the nurse promised to find her partner and reunite them.

Repeated efforts, though, failed to reach the person, who was probably home sleeping after the exhausting vigilance at the patient's bedside. The nurse worried that this might be the patient's final, brief surge of energy before passing. The nurse and her leader brainstormed how to reunite this couple. They considered contacting the city police department and asking them to make an unorthodox house call in an attempt to wake the partner. The nursing team then checked with a hospital public safety officer who concluded that the challenge was better suited for his team. So, in the middle of the night, the public safety officer made a long drive to the couple's home and awakened the patient's partner. Together, they returned to the hospital.

The couple held hands and told each other how they felt, one last time.

The story says it all. I only hope I recalled it in a way that captures the incredible act of compassion by the hospital's staff and their efforts to reunite these two individuals.

In closing, I'd like to thank these staff members and each of you for bringing your gifts, talents and passion to work throughout the year and during this holiday season.

749 + 4,452 + 137 = a lot of reasons to celebrate

My wife and I were reviewing our home calendars and the celebrations we'll share with people this month. I look forward to this time of year, the joy of the season and the opportunity to give thanks for the blessing of family, friends and colleagues. This is also a time of year when I think more often about my father. He loved the holidays and always made this time special for everyone around him. We miss him a lot.

Amid all of the holiday planning and reminiscing about family and traditions, I'm sure many staff will think about current and former patients. How many of our patients are able to celebrate this holiday season because we provided remarkable care?

Realistically, I know that there's not one exact number that answers the specific question. Novant Health team members improve health and save lives every day in our physician offices, hospitals and outpatient care centers.

I hope you'd agree that our organization is committed to quality and patient safety. We rank nationally among the best. These measurements, however, sometimes don't allow us to remember or imagine the faces of those individuals we've helped. So I asked my colleagues for some concrete numbers that convert percentages and rankings into people, real patients. I'd like to share a few "people numbers" with you.

- **749:** That's how many patients we have spared from the consequences of a hospital-acquired MRSA infection. Let me explain it another way. If we had not embarked on our hand hygiene journey in late 2005, then 749 patients would have dealt with consequences of infection with methicillin-resistant Staphylococcus aureus.

- **4,452:** This is the number of patients in our hospitals diagnosed with diabetes who had no knowledge that they had this disease prior to being admitted to a Novant Health facility. I first shared details of this Novant Health "search and rescue" mission with you in my May 14 blog, "3,050 reasons our future is bright." Since then, we've continued this screening and have diagnosed an additional 1,402 patients. With the help of physicians and diabetes educators, these individuals can now manage their disease and improve their lives.

- **137:** That's the number of patients who were kept safe from harm and avoided a serious medical error because staff used the

How many of our patients are able to celebrate this holiday season because we provided remarkable care?

five Novant Health safety behaviors and adopted a First Do No Harm culture.

All of us should rejoice after reading those numbers. And I hope you'll accept the challenge of being relentless until we can boast someday of not harming a single person.

During a period of rapid change in healthcare, one message remains consistent no matter where I visit in our organization. Many of our staff members share with me their unwavering commitment to patients. The numbers above reflect that devotion. Because of each of you, we have thousands of patients in our communities who are alive and well today, preparing to celebrate the holidays.

Section 9

The tiny picnic and making healthcare remarkable

"The best CT scan I've ever had!"

That's not something you hear every day in a medical center, but patients do occasionally make comments like that in their satisfaction surveys or in conversations with their healthcare staff.

Obviously, most individual patients don't possess the clinical credentials that would qualify them to evaluate the technical performance of the diagnostic imaging equipment or the technologists. So, what prompts that kind of comment and conclusion?

It turns out that most patients are indeed experts at CT scanning. They're consumers who are highly trained on what really matters – to them. And when patients draw conclusions about the "best IV" they've ever experienced or the "best echocardiogram," they're typically evaluating a healthcare employee's ability to perform the highly advanced technique called "listening."

As you know, we routinely survey our patients and use their feedback to evaluate how we're doing. You should be receiving routine updates about patient survey results specific to your unit or department. And if you work in a support department such as finance or IT, you should receive updates on how the health system is performing overall. If you're not receiving these updates, there's a glitch in your department.

Our patient survey system provides a lot of useful information, including clues as to which factors highly influence an individual's overall evaluation of our care and service. Not surprisingly, when patients highly rate a nurse's or physician's ability to listen carefully, those same patients rate many other aspects of their care highly. In other words, listening is a key driver – and creates a ripple effect – in creating an overall positive and remarkable experience for a patient.

Listening can take on other forms, such as anticipating a patient's concerns, watching a family member's expressions and asking questions that give you the opportunity to listen. And the skill of listening is important no matter what healthcare job you have: accountant, security officer, nurse, manager or physician.

I'd like to close by sharing part of a letter from a patient who underwent some unexpected cardiac tests. There's some great insight from this person about listening and anticipating.

"The technologist conducted my exam by talking me through every little step, in more detail than anyone else I encountered. The other staff members I met during my visit were very good and seemed authentically interested in my health. But she overwhelmed me, in a good way. Either she sensed my extreme anxiety or she anticipates it in every patient she encounters. She explained the equipment, what she was looking for, how she couldn't make a diagnosis and that an excellent cardiologist would be studying the images she was producing. She warned me about the cold gel, asked me about my comfort, and kept updating me on how much longer the exam would last. I could almost convince myself that I could perform that exam because of how thoroughly the technologist explained it to me."

That's making healthcare remarkable.

Our change of epic proportions

T hings change. And some changes are big. And then there are transformations that redefine an organization's ability to unify everyone to accomplish the most complex work ever done. That's our Dimensions electronic health record (EHR) project.

On Oct. 5, Novant Health Presbyterian Medical Center, along with the billing and registration (revenue cycle) staff, will go live with Dimensions Acute, our EHR for use in acute care facilities. This launch will be followed by Dimensions Acute implementation in our other 14 hospitals over the next two years.

This long journey began two years ago when our physician

clinics started converting from paper records to the Dimensions Ambulatory EHR developed specifically for medical offices. They've completed that project ahead of schedule. You might be one of the 185,000 patients at a Novant Health clinic who are enjoying the many benefits of the online MyChart feature.

We've matured greatly as an organization. In the past, many of us might have viewed a gargantuan task like Dimensions as an information technology services (ITS) project, led and owned by ITS management and staff. The rest of us would occupy the sidelines or relax in the stands, providing support. But today, in a health system as complex as ours, that game plan doesn't work.

ITS remains a powerful resource, but now we all own the Dimensions initiative. Our organizational value of teamwork couldn't be more evident as we have moved forward and are now ready to kick off this major strategy inside our hospitals.

Twenty-nine Dimensions Acute work groups and approximately 1,000 people are focused on this launch at Presbyterian Medical Center. That large team includes 342 additional resource personnel to assist clinicians and other team members. We studied hospitals that have experienced problems during their transition to an EHR and we've also learned from those that have succeeded. That's one reason we are launching Dimensions Acute in separate waves over the next two years, so that we can concentrate our resources and better assist staff during the conversion.

The advantages of an EHR are exhaustive:

- Portability of a patient's records

- More comprehensive patient information from clinic to hospital to outpatient centers, all in one place

- Improvements to the quality and safety of our care, including features such as EHR best practice alerts to support clinicians with decision-making

- Opportunities to make care more affordable

- Reduction of repetitive testing

- Less running around for clinicians and more time at the bedside between staff and patients

- Many other benefits

Additionally, Dimensions will serve as a powerful tool to improve communication. For instance, "electronic sticky notes" allow clinicians to message one another about issues related to patient communication, yet these notes are not a permanent part of the individual's medical record. In another example, picture a physician discussing the results of a CT scan at the patient's bedside. As the doctor studies the scan, he or she spins around the computer monitor in the room to show the patient and family the same image to point out an area of concern.

We purchased our EHR system from Epic, a world leader in this field. Yet, 60 to 70 percent of our electronic record has been developed and built by Novant Health clinicians, physician partners and other staff, to fit our unique needs.

My special thanks goes out to all of the individuals involved in this conversion – physicians, nursing staff, ITS, revenue cycle services and practically every department that comprises our health system. I hope everyone senses the excitement as we take another huge step toward delivering our promise to make healthcare remarkable.

Devastation caused by a 3-foot fall

We work in an ever-changing, dynamic field characterized by high-tech treatments and cutting-edge medical breakthroughs. Yet our industry has been forever plagued by a very simple problem – patients falling and hurting themselves in our facilities. Few effective solutions have surfaced over the decades.

An estimated 1 million patients suffer falls each year in our

… our teams adopted a loftier standard for our patients and health system.

nation's hospitals. The majority of injuries are not serious; but when they are, the long-term consequences can be devastating, especially for our older patients.

Beginning a year ago, teams of Novant Health staff emphatically pursued new solutions to decrease patient falls in our system. And they've been successful, decreasing patient falls by 77 percent. Yet, typical of our First Do No Harm culture, they're not satisfied with success or just outperforming other hospitals, even if just one of our patients falls and becomes injured.

Let me share some of the barriers they eliminated and the solutions they're introducing to accomplish the reduction.

First, the groups addressed the root of most healthcare challenges: changing the paradigm from an accepting "yes, patients do fall in hospitals" to the much more provocative response of "we must prevent that from ever happening again." The latter attitude more quickly tears down health system silos, spreads best practices and strengthens a culture that doesn't blame and instead fuels a passion to invent solutions.

Now, here are some of their specific solutions.

They're deploying data, which frequently turns out to be an effective strategy for studying a problem, determining which units and hospitals are safer than others, and then using the results to jump-start changes. We've also joined a larger national initiative to benchmark Novant Health's performance and learned that fewer patients suffer falls in our facilities than in the national sample. As I mentioned above, that's a useful starting point, but our teams adopted a loftier standard for our patients and health system.

When a fall occurs at Novant Health, the patient's care team initiates a huddle that also includes the patient and family to discuss why the accident occurred and learn what might have prevented it. We're also better at identifying high-risk patients ahead of time. These patients are asked to partner with us in their care by signing an agreement that details their role in preventing a fall, such as promising to get out of bed only with staff assistance. Some units are even stenciling a message on the room ceiling of high-risk patients, to remind them of those agreements while they're lying in bed. And the teams initiated a systemwide practice alert with six interventions to prevent falls, which included making sure that call bells are within reach and patients are wearing nonskid footwear.

Not surprisingly, many of the solutions involve addressing human behavior. Understandably, many patients struggle with modesty concerns in using the bathroom or bedpan and are reluctant to ask staff for assistance, which can result in a serious fall. And while our elderly patients are most susceptible to falls, the risk also exists for the younger, mobile individuals who are, maybe for the first time ever, recovering from injury, dealing with frustrating limitations and trying to do too much on their own while recovering in the hospital.

Some of you serve as caregivers for loved ones or counsel parents or grandparents on safety in their homes. And you might know firsthand of the devastation that can occur when someone falls, even a few feet. Preventing these accidents should be everyone's priority. I'm thankful Novant Health staff are devoted to eliminating falls and making care safer for our patients.

Mystery shoppers don't need to be sneaky

Some businesses hire professional mystery shoppers to research their services, products and customer service. It's a good strategy for certain companies.

In a healthcare organization, mystery shoppers can only conduct limited research. After all, not many people are willing to undergo surgery or diagnostic procedures "just for the experience."

At Novant Health, I believe our own team members, when they use our services as patients or visitors, possess the unique opportunity to identify ways we can improve. That's why I need you to serve as informal mystery shoppers.

When I recently met with a group of Novant Health retirees, the group asked me what they could do for our organization. They wanted to stay connected, so I asked them to evaluate our services when they used a hospital, clinic or outpatient center. I explained that they could help us achieve our promise to patients by sharing experiences and ideas for how we can improve. Now I'm asking you to do the same.

Clearly, we will better serve our patients and communities if team members are committed to finding ways to improve our own services. Think of all the times you or a family member becomes a patient. What do you notice? Was the signage helpful? Did you receive good explanations? Are there features you'd like to see added to MyChart? Are you encountering any roadblocks to getting an appointment?

Our organization continues to improve at listening to our customers and our own team members. For instance, someone suggested a Spanish version of MyChart and we're exploring that option.

I provide personal feedback on my family's experiences with Novant Health services, even if I notice more basic things, such as a cleanliness issue.

My next point is very important: Your feedback is a gift. That's how every manager or leader of a department or clinic should interpret your suggestions and observations. Sharing ideas for improvement means you care about our mission and the people we serve.

I do recognize that sharing feedback can be intimidating and out of the comfort zone for some individuals. However, try sharing examples of what went well with ideas for improvement – that can be an effective combination. You might have been impressed that a clinician shared his or her credentials and training before conducting a test or exam. Or maybe a receptionist went above and beyond to make a frail family member more comfortable. That kind of insight shines a bright light upon behaviors that others can emulate or be coached to adopt.

And remember, your feedback can help make healthcare remarkable, one idea at a time.

Telemedicine advances because we've asked, "What if?"

Some ideas need to wait for technology to catch up. Telemedicine is a good example. While the medical community has used this approach for a few applications over the past 40 years, it's now ready to play a much bigger role. Today's reliable, inexpensive and easy-to-operate video systems have made telemedicine a tool with great potential.

Telemedicine began as a way to store and forward medical images and other data to a doctor or medical specialist for assessment offline at a convenient time. Remote monitoring of vital signs became another application. And it has helped treat patients living in isolated communities who could receive care without making a long trip to see a doctor. Now, we're beginning to see expansion in its use for real-time, interactive connections between physicians and patients. Advances in technology have made telemedicine a way to close even small geographic gaps and meet patients' needs quickly and efficiently.

We see its value in clinical applications such as stroke victim identification and behavioral health determination and monitoring. For the greater Winston-Salem market, telemedicine is becoming a key part of our process for conducting behavioral health assessments of patients at all of the emergency departments. If the initial medical screening identifies the patient as possibly having behavioral health needs, a behavioral health clinician is contacted at Novant Health Forsyth Medical Center behavioral health outpatient office to conduct a teleassessment. While the assessment takes place through a video connection, an ED nurse or designee monitors the patient. Following the assessment, the behavioral health clinician documents the results, sends a recommendation to the ED and reviews plans with the ED nurse and provider for the patient's care. This process expedites the admission or referral process for the patient and allows us to share expertise at one location with many. That's telemedicine. I also think that's smart medicine.

As with any innovation, telemedicine will reach its full potential when we've asked the right "what if" questions about how we take advantage of this technology. I'm excited that we're already well on our way to using telemedicine to make healthcare more convenient and accessible for our patients.

She lived because her co-workers shared

When we use the word "transformation" at Novant Health, we're talking about dramatic change, not just a redesign of what we've done in the past. To illustrate the kind of change I'm talking about, think of personal transformations you might have experienced, such as receiving your first driver's license, starting a new career or getting married. These events result in extreme differences between how you lived before and what the future brings.

We're currently going through that kind of transformation in how we provide care across our system. As always, our goal is to improve the patient experience. And in the transformation example that I'm highlighting in this blog, it's to secure the best possible care for our critically ill and injured patients.

Critical care often involves responding to sudden organ failure and bringing patients back from the brink of death. Physicians and staff work in an unpredictable setting where a patient's status can change drastically within minutes and treatment decisions need to be made quickly. To ensure that we deliver the highest-quality, safest, most effective critical care, we need standardized plans or protocols in place that anticipate these needs and are based on solid evidence that they are the best.

Over the past two years, our critical care council and teams at several of our medical centers have been developing a set of protocols that are the building blocks of our critical care delivery model. At six of our medical centers, we're already applying this model with plans to expand to additional intensive care units this year. Our model includes protocols that reflect industry best practices and expertise we've developed and tested for years at one or a few of our locations.

An example comes from Novant Health Presbyterian Medical Center where a strong physician and nursing partnership produced a lifesaving protocol for treating septic patients. A decade ago, such patients usually didn't survive due to multiple organ failure, but the mortality rate for people coming to Presbyterian Medical Center in septic shock has surpassed industry survival expectations by 20 to 25 percent. This approach to care and team management even saved the life of one of our own.

A Novant Health team member came into the Presbyterian Medical Center emergency department in septic shock and was deteriorating rapidly. With five failed organs, she wasn't expected to live. But by excellent teamwork and following the protocol, she made it and is now back to work and living a full life.

While this example is inspiring, the story gets even better. We're replicating this kind of experience every week by

Our model includes protocols that reflect industry best practices and expertise we've developed and tested for years at one or a few of our locations.

standardizing the use of this critical care protocol and more than 20 others across our system. The result – we're gaining an amazing depth of resources. It won't matter where patients enter our system; they'll receive the highest standard of care. What great support for our brand promise!

Our critical care teams will be equipped to make timely decisions, achieve predictable outcomes and apply the full extent of their training. The patient benefits include reductions in the length of stay, ventilator use and sedation time. Most importantly, lives are saved. I can't imagine a more remarkable patient experience.

Congratulations to the critical care council and the team of physicians, nurses, pharmacists, respiratory therapists and others who truly have transformed how we deliver lifesaving services. I applaud your devotion to our patients and encourage other teams to follow your example as we transform our organization.

The 100 languages of October

The elderly gentleman had difficulty understanding directions and needed personal guidance to find X-ray. The heart patient on the fourth floor needed kosher meals. And the parents in the pediatric clinic needed a Spanish-speaking interpreter to explain what to do when their son had an asthma attack.

Our diverse patient population is growing, and it's important for us to remember that different patients have different needs. We must understand them in order to care for them. That's why "diversity and inclusion" became one of our core values; both apply to how we care for our patients and how we engage our team members, our vendors and the community at large.

Diversity is multidimensional, covering generations, cultures, races, religions, sexual orientation, gender identity and physical abilities. Inclusion encourages us to value all aspects of diversity.

Focusing on diversity means being aware of our differences, while inclusion goes further by reaching out to engage others' unique strengths and respect those differences. All of us know what it feels like to be left out and excluded, and we know how good it feels to be sought out and included.

It's our job to meet all patients where they are and make them feel good about their healthcare experience. One of our fastest-growing demographics is made up of Spanish-speaking patients. Recently, one of our physicians had a patient with a memory disorder who also had a lot of anxiety. The patient spoke Spanish, as did this particular provider, so the doctor took extra steps to answer all her questions and make her feel more comfortable.

Quality care for the patient starts with being able to communicate with the care team and understand what's going on. Hundreds of our patients need interpreters, but we don't have the capacity to have interpreters on-site 24/7, especially when you consider Novant Health interpreted more than 100 languages in the past year.

With that in mind, we are now piloting a program that uses iPads to virtually bring interpreters to the patients when and where they are needed. This gives us tremendous flexibility. We've moved from thinking about providing care for someone who is different and doesn't speak English to considering the best way to provide care for each particular patient. We've moved from embracing our differences to embedding them into our culture and into the way we do business.

October happens to be Diversity and Inclusion Awareness Month. Our team members are very much aware of diversity every day of every month throughout the year. It's who we are. When patients need an interpreter, we make sure they have one available. When patients need a kosher meal, we find it for them. When patients need help with directions, we reach out to make sure they feel welcomed and respected.

What impresses me is that, in many cases, we no longer think about how our patients are different because our team members are focused on being inclusive so that we can deliver on our mission, vision and promise – the belief that everyone who comes through our doors deserves a remarkable patient experience.

Improving a population's health starts with you

I t's amazing how far we've come in the three years since we started developing our population health model focusing on health and wellness for our team members and their dependents. For our population health goals, we are tracking 12 metrics that focus on how we are delivering value in the areas of quality, service and cost.

Our 2016 goal is that 60 percent of these metrics will be "green," meaning that we hit our targets. But more important, hitting our targets shows that we are doing the right things to deliver the best quality of care for our team members and patients. Today, I would like to talk about how the population health model can keep you and your dependents on a healthy path and about some of the metrics we track.

Good health starts with us taking care of ourselves. To do that, we all need a primary care provider (PCP). This is someone we see regularly and the person named as our provider in our health record. One population health metric tracked is how many of our team members have a PCP listed in Dimensions, because we know that people who have a PCP tend to be healthier. And for those of us who connect to MyChart, our online health record, we know the affordable convenience technology offers. We can email our PCP and schedule e-visits and video visits for some appointments. Care doesn't get much easier than that.

Then we need to take responsibility for our health. That means we get an annual well checkup, make healthy lifestyle choices and take medications as prescribed. As we build a relationship with our PCP and other providers, they're going to talk to us about our health numbers and conditions – what we might need to watch. Providers want to help us manage those conditions now before they become chronic health problems later. Our PCP will also make sure we have the needed age-appropriate screenings to ensure that we remain healthy or catch issues early. The screenings that population health is tracking this year are mammograms, Pap tests, colonoscopies, and immunizations for adolescents and children.

And if we need care but aren't sure what to do, call our team member care line. This 24/7 line includes highly trained registered nurses who can help answer any healthcare-related question: "Does my illness need treatment now? Can you help me find a PCP? Where is the closest urgent care clinic?" We also offer a variety of options so we can receive the most appropriate care in the right place at the right time. Our express care and urgent care clinics welcome walk-in appointments while offering extended and weekend hours. Receiving care at these sites also costs less than a visit to the emergency room.

Another measure we track is the number of ER visits. With any life-threatening condition, we should definitely go to the ER. But consider another option – an express or urgent care clinic – when it's appropriate. We still have some team members without a PCP who go to the ER whenever they need medical attention. This choice doesn't allow each of us to develop a long-term relationship with a provider who can tend to our individual needs.

All of these elements together impact additional population health metrics for 2016, which include patient satisfaction for our medical clinics, use of generic medications and readmission rates after a hospitalization.

Our PCP will also make sure we have the needed age-appropriate screenings to ensure that we remain healthy or catch issues early.

I'm really proud of what Novant Health has accomplished so far with our population health model, showing how we can improve access, deliver better outcomes and lower costs. With all of us working together, I'm confident 2016 will be another successful year.

Being "wired" improves the patient experience

Novant Health has long been an industry leader when it comes to harnessing technology to benefit our team and patients. In September, I traveled to Epic headquarters in Wisconsin with the Dimensions team for meetings.

During our stay, we were reminded of our recent 2015 electronic health record (EHR) achievements. Novant Health safely exchanged more than 2.6 million records with other organizations last year and 5.2 million records to date this year across all 50 states. More than 650,000 patients use MyChart, and our number of online appointments scheduled each month exceeds 10,000. Pretty impressive numbers.

Our EHR is also connected to thousands of other healthcare facilities. This year, we have already shared records with more than 900 hospitals and 24,000 clinics. We were also one of five U.S. health systems – and the first in North Carolina – to connect to the National Record Locator Service via Surescripts. Now when a patient arrives in one of our emergency rooms, urgent care clinics or physician offices, Surescripts allows the care team to access valuable clinical information from others who have previously treated the patient, regardless of where he or she received care or the type of EHR software used. By having a more complete care history, our care teams can make faster and better decisions, avoid reordering expensive tests and help ensure that our patients receive the best care possible.

Accomplishments like this prompted the American Hospital Association to recognize Novant Health this summer as a "most-wired" health system. Now that our facilities are integrated at the local and market levels, our information technology services (ITS) team continues to enhance our technology abilities at the state and national levels to improve the patient experience. We are big believers in the value of ITS, which probably puts us in the minority for health systems, but it ultimately allows us to provide a better healthcare experience for our patients.

That means we continue to reach more EHR milestones that ultimately improve the patient experience. Earlier this year, we were the first health system worldwide to be revalidated for the Health Information and Management Systems Society (HIMSS) Analytics Stage 7 Ambulatory Award for our use of an EHR. We were one of two health systems to be the first to connect to Carequality, a collaborative framework that allows us to exchange information and enhances our growing clinically integrated network.

Our technology investment continues to improve the healthcare experience for our patients. As we pursue and invest in this strategic imperative, it's rewarding for Novant Health to be recognized by others as a leader at the state and national levels in the health IT field.

Thank you to the ITS team and all that you do to make the patient experience the best it can be.

Do you always carry a spare CT injector?

When I talk about how Novant Health will grow, many people think it will be through mergers. But one way we grow and help ensure financial vitality of our organization is through shared services. With shared services, we partner with our industry peers, giving them access to our resources to help them better manage their operations or provide them with needed services. It's a way we can go on the road with what we do best.

Currently, we maintain more than 77,000 devices across a five-state region – Florida, Georgia, North Carolina, South Carolina and Virginia.

Clinical engineering, which is part of Novant Health shared services, is one of our hottest growth areas right now. Our clinical engineering team covers everything from imaging equipment repair to remote scope upkeep to instrument sharpening. Currently, we maintain more than 77,000 devices across a five-state region – Florida, Georgia, North Carolina, South Carolina and Virginia.

Hospitals can lose thousands of dollars every hour some equipment is offline. The cost of maintaining this equipment can quickly exceed its purchase price. At Novant Health, the clinical engineering team dramatically lowered those costs and we now do it for others, opening up an opportunity for Novant Health to fill a market niche.

Some partners employ our engineers on-site, but nearly a third of our highly trained biomedical technicians and radiology engineers are mobile.

One of those engineers is Lewis Frye, who spent 34 years maintaining biomedical devices at what is now Novant Health Rowan Medical Center before he transferred to field service four years ago. He wanted a new challenge and a chance to learn more, and he now specializes in repairing imaging equipment. For instance, if a broken injector takes a CT scanner down, Lewis is one of three radiology engineers available to fix it. When he gets a call, Lewis has 15 minutes to respond and he'll have a service plan in place within 30 minutes.

A couple of years ago, Lewis got a call at 6 p.m. informing him that a CT injector was broken at the Heathcote Health Center in Haymarket, Va. He hit the road early the next day from his home in Albemarle, N.C., and had the CT injector up and running by 10 a.m. That's customer service at its best. I've learned that engineers keep a spare CT injector with them at all times, so they immediately replace the broken one with their backup system once they arrive. If the broken unit can't be fixed on-site, it goes to the shop for repairs.

As you can see, shared services has tremendous growth potential. Every hospital in the country needs instruments sharpened multiple times a year, and we have a team for that. Every hospital needs scopes repaired and calibrated, and we have another team that can do that. Every hospital or freestanding imaging facility with a CT scanner will eventually have an injector break down. Lewis Frye is happy to take those clients' calls. He has traveled 160,000 miles in the last four years and he can't wait to assist others, regardless of the miles.

I see more opportunities for Novant Health to share our expertise and services with industry partners who need those solutions. And I want to thank Lewis, Denny DeNarvaez, president of Novant Health shared services, and all of our shared services team members for your commitment to Novant Health and for your service to our communities.

Intensive care can be a picnic

O ne of the things I find most satisfying about leading our organization is seeing how the good we do for patients pays dividends in their lives long after they leave our doors. That's particularly the case with some of our most fragile patients – babies cared for in a neonatal intensive care unit (NICU).

They're patients such as Bobby White, who started his life in what is now the NICU at Novant Health Presbyterian Medical Center. Bobby was born three months early and weighed less than 2 pounds. Bobby's mother, Gwen Ingram, credits the doctors and nurses at the NICU, along with constant prayer, for helping Bobby ultimately thrive.

That's why Gwen and Bobby were among the many families attending Novant Health Hemby Children's Hospital's 33rd annual NICU reunion, held earlier this month. At 26, Bobby may have the distinction of being one of the oldest NICU "graduates" to attend the event.

"Every year he goes to the NICU picnic because it's like a birthday of the hard times and trials but also the victory that came about," Gwen says of her son. "He loves seeing the doctors and nurses that took care of him."

It's the same way at Novant Health Forsyth Medical Center, Novant Health Matthews Medical Center and Novant Health Huntersville Medical Center, all of which invite former NICU or intensive care nursery patients and their families for regular reunions. Each reunion is, first, a party. The younger kids enjoy music, food and games; the families and providers reminisce and talk about milestones achieved.

But I also see events such as these as celebrations of relationships forged in trials and triumph. They are evidence of the loyalty we build with patients and their families when we give them our very best. I love the way the reunions highlight the ongoing role the Novant Health team can play in the lives of the people we serve.

When families have a baby in our special care nurseries or a NICU, the caregivers they encounter day in and day out quickly move from "stranger" to "friend." Lynn, a NICU nurse at Presbyterian Medical Center, has experienced the longevity of that caregiver-patient connection: Several of "her" NICU babies have graduated from high school and even college.

Our team has a unique opportunity to build trust and loyalty among families with babies in need of special care. But we also see that same connection-building at work in so many other areas of the care we provide, where consistently giving patients respect, compassion and attention – along with excellent care – results in relationships that span generations.

That's the way it is for Gwen Ingram. During her son's health struggles, she used to drive past the NICU picnic underway in Charlotte and promise herself that one day her child would attend.

I'm proud we can encourage long-term loyalty among patients and their families. It's exciting to know that in every encounter we have with patients, we have the chance to begin a relationship that will grow and thrive for decades to come.

Ever tried ordering oxygen at 6 p.m. on a Friday?

Over the past two weeks, I've discussed the problem of an unsustainable U.S. healthcare system that is fragmented, impersonal and expensive. Our current healthcare system focuses on how to treat illness and disease instead of working with patients to achieve better health.

Our nation faces significant challenges with heart disease, diabetes and other serious health conditions even though we're outspending all other countries on healthcare. And the cost keeps going up. It's simply unsustainable.

As consumers and providers of healthcare, we have to change the way we deliver care. So earlier this year, Novant Health introduced the patient-oriented delivery system, our answer to a flawed U.S. healthcare system. This solution puts the patient at the center of everything we do. It's our approach to population health – helping people in our communities get the right care, at the right place and at the right price in a way that delivers value to each individual we serve. Our goal is to create an epidemic of health and wellness.

For the past decade, we've been working to transform healthcare, creating a system that promotes health and helps prevent and control disease. I'm pleased that our new model is taking these efforts to an even higher level. We're now using our patient-oriented delivery model to better coordinate health services in a geographic area across multiple care settings. We call these geographic areas PODs. Today, we have PODs in north Charlotte and Winston-Salem. Further PODs go live in Northern Virginia Nov. 10 and in several other areas in the coming months.

One key to our success is the integrated team of physicians, advanced practitioners, nurses, pharmacists, social workers, dietitians, health coaches and referral coordinators, also known as the care coordination team, working together to encourage wellness and preventive care and manage existing conditions to slow or reverse the progression of disease.

There is still much work to do, but the early results provide strong encouragement that our solution works. Here's an example. A patient was discharged from acute care with an order for oxygen. When our care coordination nurse followed up with the patient at home, she learned that the oxygen hadn't been delivered to the patient's home and her oxygen level was quite low. The care coordinator called the Novant Health Inpatient Care Specialists physician who had assisted the patient and a case manager to get oxygen delivered to the patient by 6 p.m. on a Friday. The quick response likely helped avoid a readmission to the hospital.

And a patient with diabetes who had failed to start insulin injections because of a misunderstanding with his pharmacy likely avoided an emergency room visit when our care coordinator contacted him and learned what was going on. The patient quickly received the medication and instructions he needed to appropriately manage his condition.

Another key to our success is the work our physicians and clinical experts are doing around care redesign. These teams keep the patient at the center of everything we do. They are working to identify best practices that use evidence-based medicine so that we can reduce variation and leverage our capabilities and expertise. This work will change how we deliver care and will support the financial shift to a value-based model. There are more than 20 active pilots underway, including a new blood pressure program, supportive care (also known as end-of-life care), anticoagulation clinics and diabetes medication management.

To make sure you're ready to play your role in implementing our solution, visit the population health collaboration site on I-Connect. I also challenge you to get personally involved by ensuring that you are managing your own health and wellness. Visit your primary care provider for an annual checkup, make time for age-appropriate screenings such as mammograms and colonoscopies, and take time off to rest and rejuvenate because, after all, you are part of our community, too.

Consumers want "easy" and so do patients

I n a recent issue of *Forbes*, the rapid growth of urgent care clinics is attributed to the implementation of an "appealing medical model wrapped up in a proven consumer-driven business plan." Due to their convenient hours and locations, these clinics received more than 160 million visits last year. We understand the "easy for me" factors driving this trend and have many initiatives underway that apply to them. I'll review examples that you could talk about with patients, friends and family.

Through Ready At Home, we provide pharmacy services to patients in our hospitals, delivering discharge medications and other supplies at the bedside when they are preparing to leave. Our patients are able to go directly home instead of stopping at a drugstore and waiting for a half-hour or more to fill their prescriptions. They also receive education about how to properly use their medication.

Ready At Home improves the recovery of patients by ensuring they leave us with the medication and knowledge they need to adhere to their physician's care plan. Studies have found that only 75 percent of patients will stop at a drugstore following discharge to fill a prescription and then up to 35 percent of those patients don't wait for or come back to pick up their medication.

You can understand why this happens. Patients might be in pain or tired and their focus is on going home. But this decision leads to problems. The Cleveland Clinic has found the primary reason that patients with congestive heart failure are readmitted is noncompliance with medication plans. Ready At Home gives us a solution to this problem that is easy and convenient for our patients and supports value-based medicine and population health.

We're applying these principles in implementing other "easy for me" approaches, including:

- Novant Health urgent and express care facilities are now open or will soon be opened in 17 locations throughout North Carolina. They offer extended hours during the week and weekend service in convenient locations.

- Novant Health Easy Care was launched in the greater Winston-Salem market in 2013 to provide an easy-to-access, after-hours family medicine clinic.

- MyChart is a great online feature that one patient recently described as having "a doctor in my pocket." It allows patients to review medical records, schedule appointments, email their physician, request prescription refills and pay bills online.

- Self-service kiosks are available at our medical centers in the greater Charlotte market for patients to use when checking in for preregistered appointments. Patients can also use the kiosks to review insurance data, scan insurance cards, sign consent forms and make payments by credit card. These kiosks will be rolled out in other markets after they launch Dimensions.

- MyNovant.org allows new patients to find a physician or office and schedule or request an appointment online. The website also includes options to review health information, pay bills and preregister for appointments.

- Video visits are available for some of our primary care providers and we are training additional providers to offer them. These visits offer a secure, online appointment with a provider and are available within MyChart for non-emergent health concerns. All the patient needs is a computer, webcam and MyChart account.

- E-visits allow patients to fill out a questionnaire about their symptoms, submit the form to a provider and receive a recommended course of treatment without making an office visit.

- Care Now gives patients the ability to call a nurse for free medical advice 24/7.

- The Novant Health smartphone app helps find a physician, get wait times, view medical information and more.

We're working to expand these services across our system and will continue to seek additional innovative ways to deliver "easy for me" solutions. We recognize the need to make changes that keep us ahead of consumer expectations.

That's part of how we reinvent the healthcare experience to be simpler, more convenient and more affordable, so that consumers can focus on getting better and staying healthy. I appreciate the hard work of the Novant Health teams that have developed these new approaches and encourage all of you to embrace them as a chance to truly make healthcare easier for our patients.

Among the nation's best in nursing care

Today I invite you to join me in celebrating our nursing colleagues and the team members who support them. Working together, they achieved Magnet designation from the American Nurses Credentialing Center for seven Novant Health facilities. We should all feel a sense of pride in achieving this honor because only 6.9 percent of hospitals nationwide have earned it.

This achievement demonstrates our dedication to providing

They developed and maintained the highest care standards, built a culture of shared leadership and exemplified the role of nurses as leaders.

excellence in nursing services and delivering the highest quality of patient care. For the greater Winston-Salem market, it's the third designation for Novant Health Forsyth Medical Center, which is an honor that fewer than 10 U.S. hospitals have earned. Novant Health Kernersville Medical Center and Novant Health Medical Park Hospital received their first Magnet designations. In the greater Charlotte market, Novant Health Presbyterian Medical Center, Novant Health Charlotte Orthopedic Hospital, Novant Health Matthews Medical Center and Novant Health Huntersville Medical Center received Magnet redesignation.

I'm excited because the Magnet Recognition Program is the highest national credential for nursing excellence. It confirms that we're applying the right innovative and interdisciplinary approaches to addressing the healthcare needs of the communities we serve.

I had the honor of being at the Presbyterian Medical Center meeting where the Magnet redesignation for the facility was announced. I enjoyed celebrating the good news with the team that made it happen. Being named among the best in the nation required a lot of work by a wide range of team members. They developed and maintained the highest care standards, built a culture of shared leadership and exemplified the role of nurses as leaders. All of this clearly aligns with our vision to deliver the most remarkable patient experience, in every dimension, every time.

Earlier that day, I dropped into a meeting of nursing leaders as I rounded. I used the opportunity to ask for recommendations of ways to improve satisfaction for patients and team members. They suggested hiring more nurses and end-of-life caregivers and developing better ways to recruit, on-board and retain them.

Other ideas focused on more education for our front-line team members and how to involve them in the development. They also wanted to give nurses easier access to the products and tools needed for care. I appreciated receiving these suggestions and will discuss them with other leaders as we set plans for Novant Health.

Research shows that by participating in the Magnet Recognition Program we improve the care provided to our patients specifically as it relates to safety and satisfaction. It also helps recruit and retain nurses, foster a collaborative culture and advance nursing standards and practices. These benefits are good reasons to continue pursuing Magnet designations for our facilities.

I'm pleased to hear that other parts of our organization have plans to submit applications for Magnet designations. The potential applicants include Novant Health Clemmons Medical Center, Novant Health UVA Health System Prince William Medical Center, Novant Health Rowan Medical Center and Novant Health Thomasville Medical Center. I believe they will succeed and look forward to celebrating this honor again in the future. Even though the Magnet redesignation process is four years away for the seven facilities holding the honor now, efforts are already underway to achieve the continuous improvement required to qualify again.

Thanks to everyone who has contributed to our Magnet recognition. The program has my full support and I encourage all of you to do what you can to keep us among the nation's best in nursing care.

3,050 reasons why our future is bright

I will not gloss over the huge challenge ahead of us. Healthcare is going through permanent, industry-altering changes. While we might not feel comfortable admitting this fact, no one should be surprised. Over the past four years, starting with the recession and continuing with the national debate over health reform (which rages on today), almost every corner of society is asking for change. Patients, government, communities, businesses, even our own employees – everyone wants more affordable healthcare. And unlike past movements to lower what our nation spends on healthcare, the current trend has transformed into an imperative. It will never wane or go away.

Despite this unrelenting pressure to lower healthcare costs, I have recently been reminded that we can meet this national challenge and still focus on patients and their health. As a matter of fact, I received 3,050 reminders. That's the number of people in our communities who were going about their daily lives and, unbeknownst to them, had diabetes ... until our staff intervened and rescued them from a silent killer.

Novant Health staff created an aggressive early diagnosis and education program that's uncovering hospital patients who have diabetes – or are at risk of contracting the disease. Over the last 19 months, we have administered a test measuring the blood sugar control of patients admitted for any reason (except in maternity, where staff tell me that gestational diabetes risk is already closely monitored) to 11 of our hospitals. For those with elevated levels – a sign of the disease – the hospitals' diabetes educators have alerted the patients and their physicians and suggested diet, exercise and other steps that help combat the disease.

The results of this "search and rescue" mission are both sobering and uplifting. Approximately 3,050 people previously undiagnosed with type 2 diabetes were found to have the disease. Staff have told me that some patients had blood sugar levels so high they needed immediate attention before they left the hospital. And since this detection program is ongoing, the 3,050 number continues to grow with each passing week.

As most of you know, I'm not a clinician; however, my experience in healthcare has taught me about diabetes. It's a serious disease, yet millions of Americans do not realize they have it. And if undetected and unmanaged, the complications of diabetes will become severe, debilitating and fatal. That's why some staff members refer to this screening project as a "search and rescue" mission, because we're searching for hospitalized patients who had undetected diabetes, intervening, and undoubtedly rescuing many individuals from future health problems.

You should know that few hospitals in our country conduct a routine screening like this on their inpatients. We learned about this technique from a hospital in Harlem and we plan on further sharing this success with others. Keep an eye out for your local hospital's results about this screening program as we share details with staff and local media.

I'd like to congratulate the physicians, nurses and diabetes educators who teamed up to create this program. This type of initiative inspires me, especially in the midst of the local and national debate about how to lower the cost of healthcare and make it more affordable. We have the talent and commitment to succeed, at any challenge. And I know at least 3,050 reasons that support my claim.

33 individuals who would agree - safety first

Last week, I promised to begin a discussion of the five major measurements being used to see how we're doing in implementing our strategic plan. I'll start with the essential element of our plan that always comes first – safety.

We place safety at the top of our priorities because we can only create remarkable patient experiences when we First Do No Harm. Providing a safe environment for our patients and co-workers makes it possible for us to achieve our vision.

Our ultimate safety goal is to have zero serious safety events. I can't imagine that we'd ever be content to work toward anything else. To reach that performance level, we set annual targets to move us in the right direction and to do it in big steps. For

2013, we wanted to cut our number of events in half compared to the previous year. Even though we fell short of that target, we achieved a 29 percent reduction, moving from 46 to 33 events.

We use an actual number for this measurement instead of a percentage to remind us that each event involves a person – someone's father or mother, brother or sister, or friend. We've harmed a person and need to keep that in mind.

Over the past several years, we've achieved significant progress by providing safety education for all team members and making changes in areas where the frequency of events is greater than zero. We currently have four teams analyzing improvement opportunities and implementing new approaches to make us safer.

Here's a great example that involves one of our challenges – retained objects from surgery. Because of the incidence of retained cotton materials, like surgical sponges, we chartered a team to implement process improvements, education and monitoring to reduce the incidence of these retained items. The team also identified a best practice, tested it in our Charlotte facilities in 2013 and paved the way to implement it in early 2014 at all Novant Health facilities where it applies.

The technology uses radio frequency identification (RFID) markers in these materials. During surgery, patients are scanned with a device that would detect the presence of one of these markers if any materials containing them had been missed. Through this innovation, we can verify whether any of these materials remain. As you might expect, this approach results in an added expense, but it's a good investment that benefits our patients. Using RFID markers is only part of the solution and shouldn't be relied on exclusively, but it's a valuable addition to what we're doing.

We have the opportunity to reduce safety events. I'm asking each of you to think daily about what you can do to contribute to safe care for our patients. This challenge isn't limited to our caregivers. I've heard feedback from team members in nonclinical roles who realized when going through safety training that the quality of their work makes a difference in equipping caregivers with everything they need to assist patients safely. I hope you all share that recognition and will commit to doubling your efforts to improve patient safety as an essential way to achieve our vision of delivering the most remarkable patient experience, in every dimension, every time.

Taking care of the caregiver

Today, I'd like all of us to think about the responsibility caregivers have, especially when it comes to our colleagues who are caregivers at home. These individuals provide quality and compassionate care to our patients and then go home for their next round of duties: giving more medications, arranging for more doctor appointments and wading through more paperwork.

Other caregiving activities can range from checking on loved ones regularly to providing for every aspect of basic needs, from feeding to bathing to dressing. It's not only our aging parents and grandparents who will need help. Some families will care for a wounded veteran, and debilitating diseases or sudden accidents can strike loved ones at any time.

These dual responsibilities can take a toll. Novant Health is here to provide help for both patients and team members. To make it easier for caregivers, Novant Health offers both parent-to-child and adult-to-adult proxy access through MyChart. This type of access allows parents, guardians or other designated caregivers

These individuals provide quality and compassionate care to our patients and then go home for their next round of duties ...

to view important health information for a family member, friend or another individual in MyChart.

We also have a wonderful, award-winning website with a page dedicated to caregiving resources. It's a great place to learn what type of support is available. Caregivers who are struggling financially, physically or mentally will find valuable information they can use.

Last August, Rhonda, a work-life counselor with the employee assistance program, presented a Novant Health Talks on "Caregiver recharge: Managing stress, time and health." It's a must-see for all caregivers. And if you are wondering how you can help a caregiver, offering assistance is a great place to start – you can deliver a meal, volunteer your time or lend an ear.

Jan Bullard, a project manager in Novant Health marketing and communications, cared for two terminally ill loved ones in the last two years. In fact, before Jan could fully grieve her mother's death, her sister was diagnosed with late-stage cancer. It was an extremely rough road to walk.

Jan said she's deeply grateful for the professional support she had at Novant Health Forsyth Medical Center. Her family turned to Novant Health resources time and again, using case managers, palliative care, counseling, cancer nurse navigators and chaplains. "And without the support of and reaching out to resources both within Novant Health and externally, our journey would not have been as easily traveled," she said. "There was unyielding support and guidance every step of the way."

At work, we all want to make our patients' experiences easier. At home, we want to make our loved ones' experiences easier, too. Those are big responsibilities to bear. That's why Novant Health offers to help lighten the load. We have resources for colleagues who provide home care during what can be one of the hardest times in their lives. It's our mission to make healthcare remarkable! It's also the Novant Health way.

Section 10

The White House and embracing the world around us

Is the law perfect?

When our nation's government leaders passed the Affordable Care Act (ACA) two years ago, it capped an intense debate about how to best provide health coverage for more Americans and how to reform a fragmented system of care. Few laws are perfect. And the ACA is no exception.

Yesterday's Supreme Court decision will be analyzed and dissected in the days and weeks ahead because of its many ramifications. The nation will remain focused on it through the November elections, and only the state of the economy may overshadow the law during the upcoming onslaught of campaign messages.

The decision to uphold the law and individual mandate, though, does improve access to healthcare services through an intricate system of insurance reforms and other strategies.

For the most part, healthcare systems and hospitals support the law's main component: extending health coverage to 32 million uninsured people. The law contains a myriad of strategies to accomplish that expansion; needless to say, the system of expanding coverage is very complex, intensely controversial and highly political.

As healthcare providers, we support the expansion of health coverage because it creates better access to medical care for people in our neighborhoods and communities. Our physicians, nurses and other staff witness the adverse effects, every day, among uninsured patients who are not accessing primary and preventive care. As a not-for-profit healthcare system, our Novant Health hospitals, physician clinics and outpatient centers offer financial assistance and charity care to the poor and uninsured; but many people still fall through the cracks and, as a result, seek care too late or not at all.

With the guidance of the American Hospital Association,

our industry as a whole supported the ACA during the national debate. That support included a major commitment by hospitals to accept reductions in Medicare payments over a 10-year period to help pay for the expansion of coverage. The overall price tag nationally to implement the new law was estimated at $940 billion and hospitals' contribution to that effort is approximately $164 billion. The first of those reductions has already occurred at Novant Health, beginning in 2010.

So far, our health system's Medicare payments have been decreased by $6 million, and that reduction will grow to $81 million by the year 2019. Our nation's hospitals agreed to those reductions because they believe that expanding coverage and access will improve the overall health of the communities we serve. From a financial standpoint, we believe our contribution to expanding coverage may be largely offset by the benefit of having fewer people uninsured.

The law also includes other mandates and changes, but few of those will actually play a major role in truly reforming healthcare delivery. Several components of the law begin tying Medicare payments to quality indicators, such as hospital-acquired infections and patient readmission rates. We support this movement to reward high-quality healthcare, and we need to help ensure that the federal standards and data truly represent high-quality care and science-based outcomes.

In past blogs, I discussed the national and local imperative that's been given to us – to deliver the best care possible and to make our healthcare services more affordable. The Supreme Court decision does not affect our mission or our vision of delivering the remarkable patient experience and transforming care for the purpose of making it better, safer, more accessible and more affordable. We believe our communities deserve this ambition.

Nurses talk shop at the White House

F ew get invited to the White House, but I am proud to tell you that two of our own did last week. On Wednesday, two nurses had a face-to-face meeting with President Donald Trump and Seema Verma, the administrator of the Centers for Medicare and Medicaid Services, when they participated in the administration's first women in healthcare panel discussion.

After the administration asked us for participants, I suggested two team members. Invited were Lina Varela-Gonzalez, a director of nursing in the emergency department at Novant Health Presbyterian Medical Center, and Steffany Williams, a registered nurse with a critical care background from the central schedule staffing office at Novant Health UVA Health System. Steffany is also the chairwoman of nursing shared governance and of the Novant Health Professional Nurses Council. They briefly heard from President Trump who stopped by for about 10 minutes before Ms. Verma facilitated an hourlong roundtable discussion with eight women.

This wasn't a meeting about the Affordable Care Act. It was a discussion about what's going on with healthcare in our communities and states – a meeting held in our nation's capital during a week when the future of healthcare was a hot topic. Lina and Steffany said this meeting was an incredibly exciting experience, and both were impressed with how engaged Ms. Verma was as she took notes and asked questions.

Our patients and team were top of mind for both nurses. "We voiced the concerns we're seeing in the healthcare system and advocated for our patients, as well as team members," Steffany said. "We spoke about the challenges we have in creating quality care.

"It was important for me to advocate for my patients," Steffany said. "I'm hopeful that any new care act will ensure that people are able to get the healthcare that they need. We also emphasized how important it is that it's affordable care. I told them about patients I take care of who have such high out-of-pocket expense that they can't afford their care in certain instances."

Concerns about costs were also shared by Lina, who also spoke about how hard it can be for patients to access quality care. "I talked about the impact of patients not having primary care physicians and the strain that it creates on emergency services and healthcare facilities," she said. "I also touched on the mental health crisis that our nation is facing. Many of our emergency departments are becoming the place for psychiatric treatment for patients, and it affects the quality of care we provide for the behavioral health population as well as the care we provide to our community."

It's a real honor to have a seat at the table like this. The White House is looking to us to help set healthcare priorities, and it also recognizes the work Novant Health is doing at the national level.

I commend the administration for realizing how important it is to hear from women who are nurses, physicians, social workers and others closely involved in patient care. Ms. Verma's parting message was encouraging, as well. Our changing healthcare landscape is a work in progress, she said, and the participants at the table should know that the lines of communication are open. This is a conversation worth pursuing. That's why we are honored to be included. We hope to continue to capitalize on the opportunity to lend our voice to the discussion because increasing access for our patients is our No. 1 priority.

"What you do is remarkable," President Trump told the participants. I couldn't agree more. Thank you, Lina and Steffany, for advocating for our patients, representing the nursing profession and sharing our stories. You represented us well.

Make your voice heard in the voting booth

S ome of the most important things we do in life are the ones we take for granted the most. Voting can be one of those things. But the ability to choose our own leaders is a precious right, and one that many in the world don't get to exercise.

There are so many areas of life in which the people we put in office can touch our daily lives – in legislation that affects education, employment, the environment and the economy. Of course, elected officials can profoundly influence the delivery of healthcare, as well.

The exciting thing is that each of us has a voice. Never sit on the sidelines, thinking that your vote doesn't matter. It's so important that we make time to research candidates, reading from reputable sources about their views and their vision. And remember that while the presidential race naturally captures much of the attention, so many vital decisions are made at local and state levels.

No contest is unimportant. Through our choices at the polls, we have the potential to shape our communities for years to come. That's why it's a wise investment of our time to educate ourselves about the experience and skills of each candidate – and then take the knowledge with us into the voting booth.

I want to encourage each of you to make informed choices on Nov. 8. It's a tremendous privilege to have the freedom to choose our representatives in local, state and federal government. Let's exercise that right, and let our voices be heard.

No contest is unimportant. Through our choices at the polls, we have the potential to shape our communities for years to come.

Trump's first 100 days: My wish list

I've been getting asked a lot lately how I see the landscape in Washington, D.C., affecting the future of healthcare – and the path for Novant Health. The answers are complex. On the one hand, we will continue to do what we do best: going above and beyond to meet patients' needs and keep them healthy, every day. But it's true that the political climate affects the business of healthcare.

I spoke recently with Becker's ASC Review, a healthcare trade publication, about my hopes for healthcare under a Republican-led Congress and in President-elect Donald Trump's first 100 days.

I made it clear to the reporter that I am a keen supporter of the Affordable Care Act (ACA), which I believe has helped many people get the healthcare they've really needed. And I'm the first to say I was disappointed that North Carolina and Virginia opted out of expanding Medicaid coverage under the ACA, because that choice meant tens of thousands in these states were made ineligible for healthcare insurance coverage. But we made the best of the situation by encouraging as many as possible who were eligible to sign up for the care they needed, getting the word out about the Health Insurance Marketplace.

Now we face the possible elimination of the ACA. My hope is that Congress and the Trump administration will make sure the folks who got healthcare insurance through the ACA will still have it – and that if the ACA is repealed, a worthy replacement is created.

As I told Becker's, other items on my wish list include heavier investment in public health, changes to the way Medicare pays physicians, a leveling out of prescription drug increases and a fresh approach to eliminating healthcare "deserts" – places where our citizens aren't able to access the healthcare they need.

I'm also looking for new ways for healthcare systems to collaborate to make all our communities healthier. We spend a lot

What if we took some of those resources and instead used them to work together to help people get better and stay healthy?

of time and money competing with each other. What if we took some of those resources and instead used them to work together to help people get better and stay healthy? That's where, in my view, change to the current antitrust laws is needed. If we can partner with other healthcare systems without some of those barriers, think of the creativity we could unleash where it's needed most.

Those are a few of the things I'm hoping for and we're working for in the new landscape. Regardless of what changes take place outside Novant Health, what stays the same is on the inside: our commitment to delivering remarkable care and improving the lives of the people we serve.

Repositioning the national spotlight

I enjoy talking about our remarkable Novant Health team and the direction we are headed. So it was an honor to have the opportunity to share our great accomplishments on a national stage last month when I participated in a keynote panel discussion at U.S. News & World Report's Hospital of Tomorrow summit.

The CEO and president from two other innovative institutions – Brigham and Women's Hospital in Boston and Virginia Mason Health System in Seattle – joined me as we discussed Navigating a New Era in Healthcare. We talked about population health, electronic health records, physicians, partnerships, clinical transformation and the future of healthcare.

While participating in the discussion, I kept coming back to the fact that Novant Health is very progressive. People notice that we are innovative in our approach and that others have a lot to learn from Novant Health. That's why I was invited to the conference. It also helped that Jesse Cureton, our chief consumer officer, sat on a panel discussion at the summit last year and did such a good job that U.S. News & World Report wanted us back. That too says a lot about Novant Health and who we are. The story Jesse shared resonated so well that it secured us a keynote invitation for this year's conference. I'm sure that hundreds of hospital systems wanted to speak at the summit, but we were one of the few invited.

Raising our profile nationally helps us lead. The news media and the industry are interested in our story and what we do differently that sets us apart. Our ability to implement Dimensions so efficiently earned us accolades from Epic as one of its top national performers. Our nurses transformed care at the bedside by changing processes, allowing our nursing team members to practice at the top of their license and return to our patients' bedsides. As a result, this effort was profiled as the perfect transformation example in a Wall Street Journal healthcare story this summer.

While in Washington, D.C., at the summit, I also met with writers from Politico, U.S. News & World Report, Kaiser Health News, Modern Healthcare and the Los Angeles Times. The conversations were informal and not intended to lead to any immediate stories, but they did allow me to build relationships with the national press. We also know that at least one of the reporters is interested in visiting our patient-oriented delivery system and is exploring a possible story in 2015 about population health – all as a result of our conversation. In the future, these reporters will think of Novant Health when they need sources to talk about population health, partnerships in healthcare and the remarkable patient experience. These reporters cover a vast array of healthcare stories and Novant Health wants to be known as a trusted expert source across the nation.

Novant Health is in a position to be a thought leader on many topics, and the one story we own over all others is the patient experience and its importance in making healthcare remarkable. Our commitment to the remarkable patient experience seems so simple, yet it is so hard to get right in our industry. We've been committed to it for years and it is ingrained in our mission, vision, values, promise and service standards. Each of us lives it every day. That's a story all of us can share.

All eyes are on the healthcare industry across the country because everyone wants to know what healthcare is going to look like. I'm glad I had the chance to sit on a national stage and talk about what we're doing now and where we're headed in the future. Thanks to all of you for making our story a remarkable one to share!

Emerging as a healthcare leader

I think one thing is very clear: Novant Health is going to emerge as a national leader in the healthcare marketplace.

Our future success starts with the Novant Health team members we have in place now. I'm proud of our team and the remarkable care we provide our patients and our communities. At Novant Health – from the clinicians working 12-hour shifts in the hospital to the administrators in revenue cycle services to all our colleagues working at more than 380 ambulatory sites – we are delivering best-in-class care.

Many providers outside of Novant Health face the challenge of moving the gauge from "unsustainable" to "sustainable" healthcare, but it is beyond their reach. Without the right resources, they know it may be time to look at other options ... to partner with larger systems that are able to invest in better quality of care for their community. In fact, we regularly receive inquiries from smaller hospitals and systems that are seeking to join Novant Health for this very reason.

During the next year, I expect to see more partnerships and mergers across the United States. Economies of scale still exist, but to capture them, health systems need to closely monitor their operations to maintain a relentless focus on revenue growth initiatives and cost savings. And when it comes to scale, there is a strong correlation between the size of the enterprise and the strength of its credit rating. A solid credit rating provides access to less expensive capital, and Novant Health has a strong investment-grade credit rating that will provide us with the means to grow.

In the world of economics, a fragmented market creates opportunities, which is certainly true for healthcare right now. There's plenty of room for growth because, unlike many industries, healthcare remains highly fragmented, with about 5,000 hospitals and health systems operating in the United States. This fragmentation creates consolidation opportunities for larger and stronger healthcare systems, of which Novant Health is clearly one. And as we continue to grow as a system, we will see a shift from pursuing economies of scale to economies of scope and reach.

When it comes to our future, diversity will always be a factor. It's true for our team and it's also true for our partners. Similar to a stock portfolio or retirement fund, being diversified among different geographies, employment bases and payers allows us to show less variability in our cash flow margins from year to year as well as from month to month.

We are leading change in healthcare. We've already made progress in making care more affordable and accessible. We are known for our remarkable patient experience, our diversity, our quality and our teamwork. Others want to be part of our community so they can deliver best-in-class healthcare, too.

... health systems need to closely monitor their operations to maintain a relentless focus on revenue growth initiatives and cost savings.

When opportunities allow us to grow our current footprint in North Carolina, South Carolina, Georgia or Virginia, we will. You will also likely see our footprint extend to other states, as we execute on our vision of becoming the premier healthcare system serving communities located throughout the Southeast. With the great team we have in place, we are just getting started.

Recession turned more patients into shoppers

These are historic times for the healthcare industry. As we all know, healthcare in its current state is unsustainable for all participants, and major changes are ushering in a new era of healthcare.

Pushing us to change are several economic factors, and the key event that started us down the path was the Great Recession. Many businesses and families are still feeling pressure from the recession that began in late 2007, which was unlike anything we have seen in recent memory. Its severity has been sharper and deeper than any other, and six years later we are still waiting for the economy to fully rebound. Many sectors – private, business and healthcare – are still struggling with an uneven recovery and an economy that is growing slowly.

As a result of the current economic environment, growth in healthcare spending has slowed – and that affects the health system's bottom line. Many of our utilization metrics are flat year-over-year, particularly those related to inpatient services, and the growth we are experiencing is in outpatient areas where reimbursement is typically lower.

Providers are now under financial pressure to better manage their patients so they can treat the appropriate condition in the right setting. An emergency room visit costs several hundred dollars more than an office visit. That's why we closely manage our patients, especially those with chronic conditions. For instance, if we appropriately monitor the glucose levels for our patients with diabetes, then they are less likely to end up in the emergency room.

We have also welcomed a new participant to the healthcare market: the engaged consumer. Price, quality and accessibility are now more important because these well-informed individuals are deciding what their coverage will be and who will provide their care. The consumer increasingly has the final say instead of the employer. We've found some consumers are willing to trade network access for price; the smart provider will make sure it is the first choice for both categories.

This patient scenario – getting the right care in the right setting at the right price – is the future of healthcare. It's what makes healthcare affordable and it's what makes healthcare more sustainable. Many of our patients are already cared for in a more affordable environment that's easier to access. Patients can consult their primary care physician via e-visits. Nurse practitioners are available to all our patients at any time; they are a phone call away. A video session, an email or a phone call connects patients to the provider when they need to talk to that provider. It doesn't get any easier or more affordable than that. And it all enhances the remarkable patient experience at Novant Health.

We have already made changes to meet the needs of our patients as well as our payers and our communities, and we will be making more. We will find more cost-effective ways to deliver quality patient care, allowing us to make the patient experience more remarkable.

The new norm is we live in a constant state of change, and it's best for us to embrace it so we can rise to the top. The recession, financial pressures, declining reimbursements, new payment models and the rise of the engaged consumer may make us pause at first, but they ultimately make us stronger. And I'm pleased to report that Novant Health is well-positioned to turn the tide and succeed in the new state of healthcare.

The huge, quiet shift to paying for quality

We've all noticed companies that have either transformed how they meet consumer needs or turned into somewhat of a relic in our fast-changing economy. Some companies reinvented how we purchased music, at the same time that other businesses fell behind when someone else re-engineered how consumers rented movies and games.

Our industry now steps onto the same treadmill. And our health system intends to lead transformation. We're not waiting for the pace to slow down.

Today I'd like to discuss one specific facet of change we're prepared to lead. Several staff members recently calculated a very unique number: How much of Novant Health's reimbursement for the care we provide is at risk based upon our quality and safety performance? In other words, how much revenue could we lose if our quality and safety did not meet acceptable levels?

The answer: approximately $73 million in 2013. That's an incredible number, considering that it would have been practically zero about 15 years ago. This trend has been relatively quiet from a public point of view. The $73 million remains relatively small, considering it's only 2 percent of our annual reimbursements from Medicare, Medicaid, commercial insurers and other payors. Rest assured, though, that this modest percentage will increase in the immediate years ahead.

Physicians and hospital staff have been focused on quality and safety throughout our industry's history. However, in more recent years, our health system and staff have raised the bar and woven this strategic priority into our organization's very fabric. We continue every day to relentlessly explore new opportunities to provide the best care possible. Three major milestones come to mind:

1. Our medical group's participation in the Medicare demonstration project to reward high quality and efficient physician care

2. Our hand hygiene initiative to decrease patient infections

3. Adoption of our First Do No Harm culture to reduce errors that adversely affect patients

Following are a few examples of quality and safety benchmarks from a variety of payment models often referred to as pay for performance (P4P) or value-based purchasing. These criteria vary widely among government payors and insurance companies. For instance, one payor's plan contains 72 different indicators.

- The percentage of patients who acquire an infection from our facilities
- The percentage of patients who are readmitted within 30 days of their initial hospitalization for heart failure, heart attack or pneumonia
- A physician clinic's ability to e-prescribe medications
- Patient ratings of cleanliness and quietness of hospital environment
- Patient satisfaction of their communication with nurses and doctors
- Children who underwent adenoidectomies and met established criteria for having this procedure performed
- Epilepsy patients having an annual physician visit
- Adult diabetes patients who have an HbA1c test reported in the last 12 months

These criteria vary widely among government payors and insurance companies. For instance, one payor's plan contains 72 different indicators.

- The percentage of patients whose health risk is accurately assessed, coded, documented and addressed consistently across Novant Health

- Heart attack patients receiving appropriate interventions such as angioplasty within 90 minutes of arrival at the hospital

Improving the quality and safety of our care is simply the right thing to do. All of us, if we became a patient, would expect our caregivers to possess a passionate devotion to being the best. Not surprisingly, payors are now beginning to "reward" healthcare organizations that transform their passion into results.

I used quotations with the word "reward" because, in most cases, the financial incentives are actually escaping a penalty for below-average quality and safety performance. The $73 million mentioned above is not new, additional reimbursement for our services; instead, the money basically comes from existing payments that will be withheld if quality and safety standards are not met.

As a health system, we're supportive of linking payments to quality and safety criteria. Most other industries compete based upon the equation of value, cost and quality. Now it's our turn. Together, we can demonstrate how to make healthcare remarkable.

Are we good neighbors?

I promise to answer that question in this blog, but let's start with some very recent history.

When the federal government passed the Affordable Care Act, also known as health reform, the legislature included many other provisions besides the expansion of health coverage for the uninsured. Some of the less publicized inclusions were a series of requirements for tax-exempt, not-for-profit hospitals related to community benefit.

I define community benefit as the collective actions we take to improve the health of our communities, one person at a time. I hope you also recognize that explanation as our mission at Novant Health. A more expanded definition would reference all of the health outreach and services we provide our communities and neighborhoods.

So why did government add new requirements for hospitals related to community benefit? Are we not worthy of the privilege to operate as a not-for-profit organization? Are we not doing enough for the poor and the challenged of our communities? Quite frankly, these special provisions in the law, similar to a lot of new legislation, are meant to bring in line organizations that are not meeting basic expectations.

I'm confident stating that we have a long history of devoting time and resources to improve our communities, going back decades before many legislators who voted on the law were even born. We provide uninsured patients with financial assistance and charity care, which eases their burden at a time when their challenges are perhaps the most daunting. We support free medical clinics for the poor and uninsured by donating supplies, testing and other resources. We've donated buildings, land and equipment to improve the health of our neighborhoods. And staff members adopt needy families over the holidays to herald a season of giving.

Novant Health facilities and staff engage their communities. A few years back, an energized group of staffers asked me to participate in building a new playground for a deserving neighborhood. Novant Health Thomasville Medical Center provides personal care items to students in need, including soap, deodorant, shampoo and other basic hygiene items many of us would take for granted.

Novant Health Rowan Medical Center partnered with local community schools to offer Fit for Motion, a program designed to prevent childhood obesity by educating second-graders about the importance of regular exercise and good nutrition. The following note came from a hospital nurse who encountered one of the second-graders impacted by this program: "I was treating a little boy after school who was really excited about his day. He said he had extra money in his lunch account and was able to get something extra to eat that day. I figured he would say he got cake or ice cream or something like that. He said, 'No, I got an extra helping of green beans and they were so good!' I asked him where he had learned such wonderful healthy behavior. He replied that there was a really nice man who came to his school who taught them about good eating habits during Fit for Motion."

I could list hundreds of examples from around our health system. As a matter of fact, Novant Health staff is in the process of taking inventory of all of our community benefit programs, which is an important step in making sure we can effectively share our story about community outreach and our efforts to improve health.

While the new law is intended to hold not-for-profit hospitals more accountable for meeting community needs, Novant Health embraces this change as an opportunity to continue our tradition of helping others and to communicate that passion to legislators, patients, the public and our own staff. Thanks for all you do to improve the healthcare needs of our communities.

Friends like tweeting the mayor after yelping

When it comes to social media, my children are much savvier with these modern-day communication tools. I'm learning, but slowly. Twitter, Facebook, Foursquare, Pinterest, YouTube, LinkedIn, Instagram, Yelp – the list keeps growing and I keep trying to follow these trends and new communication resources.

Facebook "friends" decide to "like" your new "post." Someone "pinned" a favorite recipe and another person "repinned" it. An active user of Foursquare achieves the status of "mayor" ... all this jargon and activity can be both exciting and exasperating, depending upon a person's interest in social media. For me personally, I'm pledging to improve my knowledge base of social media, but my progress has been slow.

Novant Health now employs several staff dedicated to implementing social media opportunities for our organizations, our patients and communities. This communication specialty has become a basic skill set needed by healthcare systems, just like we need experts in electronic health records and website development.

One recent story epitomizes the value and power of social media. Bonnie was just 1 pound, 8 ounces when she was born in 1973 and cared for in one of our neonatal intensive care units. She's now middle age and thriving, thanks to the remarkable care she received four decades ago. Bonnie reached out to us through our hospital Facebook page because she wanted to thank her doctors and nurses and let everyone know how grateful she still is to them for saving her life. What a moving gesture after such a long time. Bonnie currently resides along the Gulf Coast where she has lived since she was 1 year old.

Bonnie's parents moved to North Carolina almost 40 years ago specifically for her birth, as they knew that their baby would arrive prematurely. They were told that our communities had outstanding care for critically ill newborns, and they wanted Bonnie to have the best chance at survival.

Her contact with us through Facebook highlights how social media connects people in ways that are personal and expressive. Our health system continues to explore and expand uses of social media. For instance, Novant Health UVA Health System Prince William Medical Center recently posted a new photo gallery on Facebook about the construction of its new community hospital in Haymarket. The result – 32,232 saw the communication. Novant Health Brunswick Medical Center, with family permission, posted photos on Facebook of a wedding performed in its chapel at the bride's and groom's request, so that a hospitalized loved one could attend the ceremony.

... social media provides powerful and resonant opportunities for sharing and accessing information important to their health and overall well-being.

I realize that many individuals are slow adopters of social media and that others will never explore these new communication phenomenons. For many of our patients and staff, though, social media provides powerful and resonant opportunities for sharing and accessing information important to their health and overall well-being. And these new media provide an excellent opportunity to develop a more authentic, personalized relationship with people.

"I'd like one forklift full of syringes, please"

When I walk into a Costco or Sam's Club, it's easy to recognize the popularity of these stores. The success of their businesses certainly acknowledges the value of buying supplies and necessities in bulk. Fresh produce, canned goods, flat-screen TVs – prices come down when the quantities go up.

Several weeks ago in my blog, I shared my thoughts about the advantages of growing larger as a health system. One of those advantages included improving our economies of scale when purchasing supplies. I'd like to further describe some of Novant Health's newest efforts to lower what we pay for supplies. In healthcare, we used to label these programs as "purchasing" or "materials management." Today, we refer to the process as "supply chain" or "strategic sourcing," which more accurately describes the more integrated approach we use for buying healthcare goods and materials.

Our health system purchases a tremendous volume of supplies each year. For instance, our logistics center in Kannapolis distributed 9,150,202 syringes to our facilities last year. Overall, we have approximately 200 staff members devoted to buying and distributing supplies to our nursing units, clinics and departments over a three-state area. Hundreds of other staff members are also involved throughout Novant Health – they're the individuals who use these products and services and help our supply chain personnel evaluate what we purchase to ensure quality and safety, as well as affordability.

In the past six years, our increased efforts to purchase supplies and services more economically have produced $181 million in savings. On an annual basis, we reached $52 million of savings in 2011, which included substantial savings in areas such as orthopedic implants, cardiac medical devices, contrast media used in diagnostic imaging procedures, food, office supplies and pharmacy. And our annual savings will increase as we grow as a company and become even more creative with our supply chain program.

Did you know that Novant Health formed a supply chain company together with two other health systems that are each as large as our organization? It's a good example of the innovation taking place. We helped form that new company about 10 months ago by joining forces with Sentara Healthcare and MedStar Health. Sentara's concentration of facilities is located in southeast Virginia and MedStar's are centralized in the Baltimore and Washington, D.C., area.

The main purpose of this company is to pool together our supply purchases in order to lower the prices our three organizations pay for items. For example, Novant Health recently saved approximately $550,000 when the three health systems purchased computers together. We informed three major vendors about the number of computers we wanted to buy, and they aggressively bid online for the business. To describe this advantage another way, if Novant Health had purchased the computers on our own instead of in conjunction with Sentara and MedStar, we would have spent $550,000 more. In another example, Novant

Health recently saved $1 million a year by purchasing vaccines together with the other two health systems. And the list of opportunities will continue to grow. We've established a two-year goal of saving $36 million for the three health systems that formed this new company.

These supply chain savings are critically important to our health system as we prioritize delivering the remarkable patient experience and making our healthcare services more affordable. These savings help us provide care to those in need in our communities, acquire new technology, renovate our facilities and invest in our people. And as we grow as a health system, we can expect our strategic sourcing advantage to improve.

One hospital's local quest addresses a national crisis

The entire fourth floor of Novant Health Thomasville Medical Center represents a success story about meeting an important healthcare need while also strengthening a community and its hospital.

The hospital joined Novant Health in 1997. At that time, Thomasville leaders concluded that its local medical center could better serve its patients and communities by partnering with a larger healthcare organization. Since that time, the city of Thomasville and the surrounding county area have gone through changes like many rural areas, with ups and downs in the economy.

The hospital, situated in the furniture hub of America, has made a lot of changes over the past decade, but probably none more significant than in 2002 when it opened a 15-bed geriatric behavioral health unit.

To jump ahead to the final chapter of this success story, the specialty unit that serves older adults experiencing mental health problems has grown rapidly, most recently expanding for the third time to reach its current capacity of 45 beds, each time adding jobs in the community. The unit now employs 100.

More importantly, the geriatric behavioral health unit has met a critical need. Many experts consider mental health in "crisis" locally, statewide and nationally, plagued by severe access problems. The Thomasville program is playing a humble role in helping address part of the crisis; the geriatric unit frequently operates near capacity and sometimes individuals cannot be admitted to the busy specialty unit when beds are not available. Patients from all over North Carolina – from the coast to the mountains – receive care at the specialty unit. Some patients travel there from out of state.

Older adults are prone to depression, anxiety disorders and cognitive impairments such as Alzheimer's disease and other types of dementia. Their treatment often is complicated by physical illnesses and the array of medications they take. The average length of stay in geriatric units is 12 to 14 days, longer than in other adult psychiatric wards, because it takes longer to stabilize and treat older patients with psychiatric issues.

Research shows patients receive more complete medical work-ups and cognitive assessments, better monitoring of drug dosages and side effects, and more comprehensive aftercare referrals in specialized geriatric units.

We're all familiar with the accelerating trend of our aging society and the responsibility of our nation to prioritize the healthcare needs of senior citizens. Our parents and grandparents, and each of us someday, deserve access to the best care possible. Thomasville Medical Center's program is helping fulfill that expectation.

Sharing our stories on social media

If you have watched the video, it's impossible to forget: a smiling 6-year-old who arrives each week for cancer treatment at the St. Jude Affiliate Clinic at Novant Health Hemby Children's Hospital – ready to dance.

I've been touched by the story of pediatric cancer patient Braylon Beam, who is joined by his family and the clinic team in wacky weekly dance parties. It's a story that's led to a People.com article on Braylon and his family and to their appearance on *The Ellen DeGeneres Show*.

And it's a story that came to the public's attention through the power of public relations and social media.

This organization is full of amazing stories – stories of health restored, of hope renewed. We're also a kind of living library of healthcare information, with clinicians who have years of knowledge on how to get better and stay healthy.

More than ever, our public relations team is using social media to share those stories and that knowledge with our communities. Our providers are weighing in on healthcare issues of the day on our Healthy Headlines site. Recent stories there have addressed everything from seasonal allergies to postpartum depression, and we share these articles on social media, as well. We're getting the word out about Novant Health's community events on Twitter. And we're sharing remarkable stories such as Braylon's on our Facebook pages.

Novant Health needs to be active on social media because that's where our customers are. Not only that, but I believe that social media allows us to tell our story in a way that is more organic, more transparent. It allows us to become that trusted source in our communities by building an authentic relationship with our followers.

And, as we all know, news shared on social media spreads with astonishing speed. When our public relations team created a short, upbeat video of Braylon showing off his dance moves and posted it to the Novant Health Facebook page and others, in just one weekend, it went from 1,000 views to more than 9,000. That's how powerful person-to-person sharing of a story or video can be.

And you can be a part of that experience. For those of you who use Facebook or Twitter at home, I would ask you to follow

Novant Health and share our posted stories with your family and friends. As ambassadors of our brand in our communities, you can help us extend our reach significantly while helping spread messages of health, wellness and remarkable care.

The story of an amazing little boy determined to choose joy in the face of his healthcare challenges has resonated with so many. And we're looking forward to using social media to share both expertise and inspiration with many more.

Giving to our neighbors, colleagues, communities

The chances of survival of a critically ill patient at Novant Health Rowan Medical Center were increased with the use of a new Site-Rite Ultrasound machine. A little boy in Winston-Salem was expected never to walk or talk – but is making great strides thanks to help from the United Way-supported Children's Center. And a team member in Charlotte needed a helping hand after a home-destroying fire.

Who helped make the difference in each of these situations? You did.

Your gifts during our annual *Giving. Serving. Together.* campaign last year directly aided these people and hundreds more in Novant Health's communities. This year's opportunity to help runs from Sept. 21 through Oct. 30. The money we contribute funds everything from crucial hospital equipment purchases and help to team members in crisis to humanitarian assistance in our communities. You can write a check or choose payroll deduction; and this year, you'll see new giving choices in each market. You'll soon be hearing details from your fellow team members, who will be encouraging you to make your pledge on self-service.

I know that many of us already contribute to charity by giving directly to organizations or to houses of worship. That generosity makes the world a better place. I'm asking each of you to also consider giving through this campaign.

Here's why: We at Novant Health, in all of the places we serve, are part of an economic ecosystem. We have a responsibility to make our foundations and agencies in our communities as strong as they can be. Those groups support our neighbors and team members, and often they wind up giving back to us.

Let me share another way in which you helped transform lives through last year's campaign.

Some of you know what it's like to come from a family that lives on the financial edge, with never quite enough food in the cupboard. That kind of hunger is often hidden in our communities, but it's there. Last year, your donations helped Communities in Schools of Rowan County feed more than 970 students and their families, by filling kids' backpacks with food. Think about it: Boys and girls who get by during the week on meals at school – but who face weekends of empty stomachs – brought food home to their families, in part thanks to you.

We all have blessings we can share with others. We have it in our power today to make our communities more vibrant and beautiful and the people who live in them safer and healthier.

Any amount makes a real difference. If we, as a team of 26,000, saw each team member contributing $2 per pay period, it would make a tremendous impact on our communities. Let's work together to help others! Thank you!

Finding our global voice for women's healthcare

The world is moving toward globalization, and we want to be a part of that. So I'm excited about recent recognition for our women's wellness center in the greater Winston-Salem market – which is expanding its mission to help women live longer, healthier lives.

Recently, the United Nations granted special consultative status to Novant Health. What this means is that our providers and team members will consult with other experts on the most important local and global issues involving women's and girls' health. This chance to work with the U.N. Economic and Social Council adds an international dimension to our commitment to improve the health of communities, one person at a time.

Along with this consulting role comes a big responsibility. Think about this. Our mission, vision and values call on us to think in inclusive ways about everything we do. This means everything from the way we engage with our team members to how we deliver remarkable care to our patients, and even to the way we define our communities. That is why we must have the courage to say and do something about the healthcare needs we see, not only in our markets, but also in ZIP codes and regions elsewhere. We have an opportunity to bring a compassionate voice to the healthcare needs of women around the world who face very challenging circumstances, such as living great distances from clinics or having limited access to safe childbirth care.

These scenarios are familiar to the Maya Angelou Women's Health & Wellness Center at Novant Health Forsyth Medical Center, which applied for the U.N. consultative status on behalf of our organization. The goal of the center – established in 2012 by Kirsten Royster, president and chief operating officer of Novant Health Medical Park Hospital, and Chere Gregory, MD, senior vice president of women's services – is to improve women's health locally, nationally and globally. In fact, Dr. Gregory has spoken twice at U.N. conferences on women's healthcare needs.

As part of their on-the-ground work, our team members and providers travel internationally to work alongside clinical providers within their countries. One of the ways this happens is through the center's partnership with Kybele, Inc., a nonprofit organization devoted to preventing childbirth-related injury and death. Kybele's

The goal of the center ... is to improve women's health locally, nationally and globally.

president, Medge Owen, MD, is an obstetrical anesthesiologist and medical director of global health programs at Forsyth Medical Center.

Years ago, Dr. Gregory met with Maya Angelou to talk about naming the center as part of her legacy. She remembers the way the late poet, author and Winston-Salem resident took delight in how the center's vision matched her own expansive definition of community.

"When the hale and hearty gather to improve the condition of the ailing and the weak, the entire community is inspired and the needy are cared for," Ms. Angelou said when the center opened. Ms. Angelou wanted to be sure we would focus on people without power and without voice. We can find women and girls like that everywhere. Let's congratulate our team members from obstetrics and gynecology, women's services and our medical group for changing lives for the better not only in our region – but also around the world.

Transforming our communities, one life at a time

I often hear team members say that they're proud to work for Novant Health, especially when it comes to caring for those in deep need. I am, too. All work is worthwhile. But the work of mending bodies, healing hurts and keeping people well – that's beyond mere work. That's a mission.

As a not-for-profit healthcare system, we offer that same help to people regardless of their ability to pay. We extend a financial assistance policy – one cited by a study as above-and-beyond generous – to our friends and neighbors in need. We also offer everything from free screenings to education to support groups. It's what we call "community benefit," and it's part of our identity.

We serve our neighbors in this way in part because we are only as strong as the region around us. But more important, our purpose is to improve the health of entire communities, one person at a time. We address disparities in access to healthcare, change the course of chronic disease and prevent illness through early intervention. It is never enough to treat people who walk in your door already sick. To truly be leaders, we move outside our hospital and clinic walls into neighborhoods, schools, houses of worship and community centers to foster wellness and help people lead the healthy lives they deserve.

As I read the 2016 Novant Health community benefit report, I was struck by the fact that behind every program, there's a person. Some we know by name, like Barbara, a Clemmons resident who struggled with her weight. She knew that without intervention, she likely faced an unhealthy future. She enrolled in our program aimed at achieving a healthy weight, a class whose costs were covered in part by our community benefit. Barbara told us that the class taught her "a new way of life."

And there are so many others we don't know by name, but it doesn't take much imagination to picture them. The women in the Raleigh area who received what, in some cases, were lifesaving heart screenings through Novant Health's work with the American Heart Association. The families in Haymarket who have access to healthy, local produce thanks to our help sponsoring a farmers market at our medical center. The babies in Brunswick County who will get much-needed supplies because we threw a community baby shower for moms in need.

The key point is this: In ways large and small, we are lifting people from want to wellness.

Maybe you, like me, have done a lot of different jobs over the course of your career. But I've got to tell you, nothing equals the satisfaction of leaving this world better than you found it, of extending a hand to someone in need, of changing human lives. Novant Health doesn't provide a community benefit so it can check a box. We enrich communities for one simple reason: It is the right thing to do.

Be proud of that. I know I am.

Carl S. Armato is president and CEO of Novant
Health, one of our nation's largest and most respected healthcare organizations. He joined the organization in 1998 as the vice president of finance and operations for the physician division. Carl was promoted to other Novant Health leadership roles before becoming the health system's top executive in 2012. His career in healthcare management began in Louisiana, where he was born and raised. Carl serves in other professional and civic roles, both locally and nationally.

He credits his parents for teaching him about the value of a strong work ethic and connecting to a community and its people. Since Carl's first job as a grocery store clerk, he has woven those early lessons into his family life, career and public service.

Novant Health is a not-for-profit integrated system composed of hospitals, physician offices, outpatient surgery centers, medical plazas, rehabilitation programs, diagnostic imaging centers and community health outreach programs. The health system and its staff serve patients in North Carolina, Virginia, South Carolina and Georgia.

Thanks to the organization's talented team members, Novant Health is nationally recognized for its quality of patient care, safety, disease management and customer service. Its mission is to "improve the health of our communities, one patient at a time."